THE NEW MERMAIDS

The Shoemaker's Holiday

THE NEW MERMAIDS

General Editor

BRIAN GIBBONS

Professor of English Literature, University of Zürich

The Shoemaker's Holiday

THOMAS DEKKER

Edited by

ANTHONY PARR

Lecturer in English
King's College, London

LONDON/A & C BLACK

NEW YORK/W W NORTON

Second Edition 1990
A & C Black (Publishers) Limited
35 Bedford Row, London WC1R 4JH

ISBN 0-7136-3288-7

© *1990 A & C Black (Publishers) Limited*

First published in this form 1975
by Ernest Benn Limited

© *1975 Ernest Benn Limited*

A CIP catalogue record for this book
is available from the British Library.

Published in the United States of America by
W. W. Norton & Company Inc.
500 Fifth Avenue, New York, NY 10110

ISBN 0-393-90062-2

Printed in Great Britain by
Page Bros (Norwich) Ltd.

ACKNOWLEDGEMENTS

For help in preparing this edition I would like to thank Simon
Blatherwick, Nat Brenner, Brian Gibbons, Margaret Parker, Derek
Seeley, Anne Watts and Sue Winter. I am also indebted to the
excellent Revels edition of the play by R. L. Smallwood and Stanley
Wells (Manchester, 1979).

A.N.P.

CONTENTS

**IN MEMORY OF
BERNARD HARRIS**

INTRODUCTION

THE AUTHOR

VERY LITTLE is known of Dekker's life, but he was one of the most prolific writers of his time and the general shape of his career can be inferred from theatrical records and the part of his huge output which has survived. Dekker probably began writing for the theatre in the earlier 1590s (when he had a hand, along with Shakespeare and others, in the unpublished play *Sir Thomas More*); and by 1598, when in his mid-twenties, he was established as one of a group of writers employed by the impresario Philip Henslowe to supply the repertory of the Admiral's Men, the acting company whose principal venue was the Rose Theatre on Bankside. These writers did not, as did Shakespeare, have the advantage of a shareholding in the theatres for which they worked; they were jobbing dramatists, paid for each play produced, and they usually had to work at high speed, frequently in collaboration, in order to make a living and satisfy the demand for new plays. Dekker was notably versatile under pressure: in the year he wrote *The Shoemaker's Holiday* he also worked on several tragedies and history plays (none of which has survived) and completed two other comedies, *Patient Grissil* (written with Henry Chettle and William Haughton) and *Old Fortunatus*. But although he always found a market for his work it did not bring him financial security. In 1598 and again in 1599 Dekker was in prison for debt, and on both occasions Henslowe had to advance the money to obtain his release. Later such help was not forthcoming: Dekker languished in gaol for seven years, from 1612 to 1619, and he apparently died in debt in 1632, since his widow renounced the administration of his estate, presumably to avoid inheriting liabilities. Dekker may have been unusually incompetent at managing his finances, but his personal difficulties seem to have made him particularly sensitive to the poverty and insecurity that surrounded him at a time of rapid social change. Even in the relatively buoyant atmosphere of the late 1590s, when national confidence was high and the old Queen was felt to preside over decades of achievement, Dekker had reason to be aware that life for many was precarious, however hard they worked. That knowledge is woven into the generally optimistic fabric of *The Shoemaker's Holiday*.

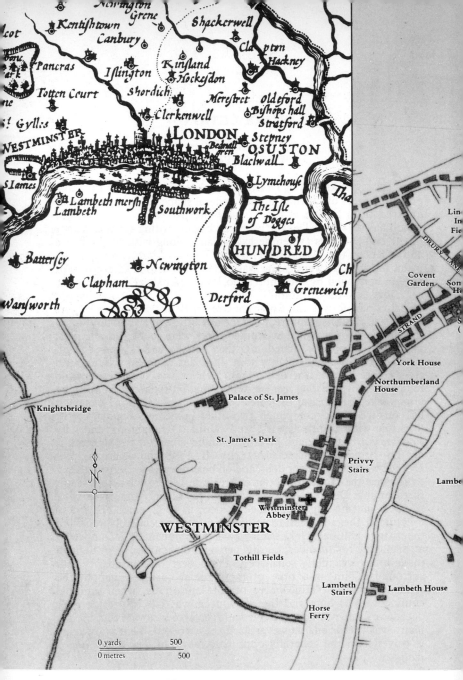

Inset map is a detail from Norden's Map of Middlesex with the Cities of London and Westminster. It shows the position of Islington and Old Ford. (Reproduced by kind permission of the Museum of London)

The modern map of Elizabethan London shows several of the playhouses marked. (Drawn by John Plower and based on that in *Literary Landscapes of the British Isles* Published by Bell & Hyman)

After the turn of the century Dekker continued to write for the theatre, collaborating with most of his major contemporaries, Middleton, Webster and Ford among them; and he also embarked on a career in what we would now call journalism, producing topical pamphlets, light fiction, satire, and verse to commemorate special occasions. In 1603 he was commissioned by the City of London (with Ben Jonson) to write a civic pageant for the arrival of King James, and in his later years he created similar events to welcome the incoming Lord Mayor. Dekker was in every sense a popular writer, and his work is always somehow addressed to the problems and aspirations of citizens and working people in his native city. The primary fact in Dekker's biography, and the only really important one, is that he was a Londoner. His name suggests that he may have been of Dutch ancestry, and there are elements in his work – such as Lacy's disguise – to support this; but he was born and raised in London and identified very closely with the city, whether in celebrating its civic achievements or in lamenting the poverty, crime and disease endemic in urban life at this time. Dekker's 1603 pamphlet *The Wonderful Year* commemorates London's worst outbreak of plague in living memory, when 30,000 people died; and in what he called his 'picture of London, lying sick of the plague', and in subsequent works like *News from Hell* and *The Seven Deadly Sins of London* (both 1606), and *Lanthorn and Candlelight* (1608), the city becomes a focus for his exploration of social and moral issues. The exploration is less intense in *The Shoemaker's Holiday*, and the anguish over deprivation and suffering much less evident; but Dekker's engagement with London in this early play declares the creative confidence of the writer who has discovered his true subject.

DATE AND SOURCES

The date and authorship of *The Shoemaker's Holiday* are established by an entry in Henslowe's diary for 15 July 1599, recording a payment of three pounds (assumed to be the second and final payment) for 'A Boocke of thomas dickers Called the gentle Craft'. As noted above, Dekker was very active in that year, and the play was probably written quickly during the weeks preceding its purchase for the Admiral's Men. It is likely that it was first performed at the Rose Theatre in the late summer or autumn of 1599.

Dekker's principal source for the play was Part One of Thomas Deloney's *The Gentle Craft*, a collection of stories celebrating the trade of shoemaking and 'shewing what famous men have beene

Shoomakers in time past in this Land, with their worthy deeds and great Hospitality.' The book is thought to have been first published in 1597, but no copies of the earliest editions have survived, doubtless because they were read to pieces. The first story is that of St Hugh, the patron saint of shoemakers, to whom Dekker alludes at several points in the play (see commentary note to 4. 46); but his direct borrowing from Deloney is confined to the second and third tales, which relate, respectively, the adventures of the royal brothers Crispine and Crispianus and the rise of Simon Eyre. The Crispine-Crispianus story is set in Roman Britain and concerns two princes who become shoemakers to escape the tyranny of the Emperor Maximinus. In due course Crispine secretly marries the Emperor's daughter, while Crispianus is pressed to the wars in France, where he covers himself in glory. Crispine's adventures are the basis of the Rose-Lacy plot, and Dekker reshaped and divided the role of Crispianus to provide Lacy with a companion, Askew, who goes to France in his place, and a working-class foil in Ralph, who like Crispianus is forced to serve as a soldier but unlike him comes home a cripple.

Deloney's third story – the rise of Eyre – provides the backbone of the play but Dekker makes some important changes. His characterisation of Eyre owes little to Deloney's sober and conventional citizen, and the same can be said of the portrayal of Eyre's wife, who is transformed from a shrewd and ambitious city dame into the idiosyncratic Margery of the play. In Deloney, Eyre's wife is the moving force behind the plan to buy the ship's cargo, persuading her husband to an act of outright deception in dressing up as a alderman so that he can obtain the necessary credit. Dekker truncates the episode, apparently seeking to play down its dubious legality, and renders it more wholesome by avoiding the theme of wifely ambition and instead having Eyre's transaction made possible by a generous loan from Lacy, who in his disguise as Hans also handles negotiations with the Dutch skipper. In this way the episode not only advances Eyre's fortunes but develops his relationship with Lacy and helps to motivate Eyre's later intervention to save the young man from disgrace.

Dekker's portrayal of Eyre's workshop takes its cue from Deloney's frequent testimonials to the generosity, high spirits and good fellowship of the shoemakers (songs figure prominently in both story and play); though the sharply delineated figures of Firk and Hodge are entirely his invention. He may also have been influenced by Deloney's decision to intercut the narrative of Eyre's rise to power with a comic-romantic intrigue involving three of his journeymen and Florence, a maid in the Eyre household. This provided a number of hints for the play, including a Dutchman called Haunce and an interrupted wedding; but the way in which Dekker integrates his two love plots into the main action produces a quite different overall effect, and in any case probably owes more to the conventions of multiple plotting already established in English dramatic writing.

THE PLAY

To turn Deloney's tales into effective theatre, Dekker needed a structure that would resolve incompatibilities between the two stories he was using and give the action a firm shape, with the separate plot lines ultimately converging in resolution. His material presented certain problems in this respect, the first being that the story of Simon Eyre was in some ways not particularly suited to dramatic treatment. Deloney chronicles a series of episodes in a successful but by no means meteoric career (the historical Eyre, who lived in the mid-fifteenth century, only became Lord Mayor eleven years after being sheriff), and the story generally lacks impetus and immediacy. Dekker had to find a way of conveying the inexorable quality of Eyre's rise, not allowing dramatic tension to evaporate between the stages of his success, without at the same time making it seem implausibly rapid. He does this, firstly, by concentrating not on Eyre's formal attainment of office (there are no scenes of investiture in the play) but rather on its social anticipation and aftermath – the noisy pride of his workers, Margery's fussing over wigs and farthingales, and above all Eyre's own instinct for the big occasion. Theatrically speaking, Eyre's greatest achievement is his own personality, and the dominant impression left by the play is one of expansion, not of progress in a straight line, as Eyre generates out of himself the festive mood which gradually comes to dominate the entire action.

Meanwhile, Dekker is careful to tell us that 'seven of the aldermen be dead, or very sick' (13.35–6), thus facilitating Eyre's election as Lord Mayor; and by having him succeed Oatley in that office he fosters the idea of narrow, snobbish officialdom yielding irresistibly to the tenure of the public-spirited man. But the exposition of Eyre's career is also regulated by the two sub-plots. In the case of the Rose-Lacy story, Dekker brings the romantic fable he found in Deloney within the orbit of the main plot by setting the entire action in and around London and locating the lovers' difficulties in the kind of class conflict and intolerance that Eyre's influence gradually dispels. His success and that of the lovers become mutually reinforcing, joint products of a generous and unfettered social ethos. The Ralph-Jane plot, which has no counterpart in Dekker's source, has a rather different bearing on Eyre's fortunes. Partly this is because the predicament of Ralph and Jane is much more intractable, stemming from economic and political realities which they and Eyre are equally powerless to influence. Although husband and wife are part of the Eyre establishment, he is unable to stop Ralph being conscripted, and later in the play we learn that Jane has left his house in ambiguous circumstances, as related by Margery:

> ... we know not what's become of her. She was here a while, and because she was married grew more stately than became her. I checked her, and so forth. Away she flung ...   (10. 84–7)

Whether we trust Margery's account or not, it forces us to see Eyre's establishment not as an ideal haven (as it mostly is for Lacy) but as a demanding environment where Jane can expect no special consideration. Fundamentally it is only good fortune that brings Ralph and Jane together again, and we do not forget this even when the shoemakers unite behind Ralph in a mission to rescue Jane from marriage to Hammon. The stirring confrontation with the wedding party in Scene 18 is obviously calculated to make the audience side with the shoemakers and applaud their victory; nonetheless Dekker does not associate Eyre with their rough tactics, and avoids the easy implication that the reunion of husband and wife is merely a holiday achievement (though it owes something to the fraternal solidarity Eyre inspires in his men). Instead, the Ralph-Jane plot gives a realistic edge to the play, and deepens and complicates our sense of the workaday world in which Eyre steadily enlarges his authority.

The story of Ralph and Jane lends the action of the play a notable symmetry, balancing the Rose-Lacy plot in a number of ways. Both men work for Eyre, both relationships are challenged by the same rival, both are affected by national events; but these structural parallels often contain an ironic social comment. This is apparent at the start when Lacy bribes Askew to cover his absence from the French wars, and then pulls rank to remind Jane and Ralph of their obligations:

> Woman, be patient; God no doubt will send
> Thy husband safe again, but he must go:
> His country's quarrel says it must be so.   (1. 181–3)

The link between class and self-determination is again highlighted when Hammon appears on the scene and threatens each relationship in turn: he makes no progress with Rose, protected as she is by social position and the supportive Sybil, but eventually he is able to exploit Jane's poverty and friendlessness, which make her vulnerable in spite of her evident integrity. Neither of the love plots is extensively dramatised, and indeed Dekker chooses not to present several key events, such as the wedding of Rose and Lacy and the betrothal of Jane and Hammon. In both instances the intention seems to be to reserve the main emphasis for the abortive wedding episode in Scene 18 which, through Firk's ingenuity (see 16.146–52), is the means by which both love-plots are to be resolved. This may also be the reason why Dekker does not show but has Ralph describe the scene where, unrecognised by his wife, he fits Jane's wedding shoes:

> I looked upon her, and she upon me, and sighed, asked me if ever I knew one Ralph. Yes, said I. For his sake, said she – tears standing in her eyes – and for thou art somewhat like him, spend this piece of gold. I took it; my lame leg and my travel beyond sea made me unknown.
>
> (18.8–12)

But Dekker is also aware of how effective in drama a reported incident can be, and in the lull before the confrontation with Hammon the simplicity of this past-tense narration, with its hint of an opportunity missed, is particularly moving. Its impact is enhanced by our recollection of a comparable incident in Scene 15, where Lacy, reunited with Rose, is forced by Oatley's unexpected approach to improvise and play the shoemaker, pulling on Rose's shoe. Acted out, the episode is bawdy and romantic, with a touch of farce, guaranteeing for this pair of lovers the happy ending which for Ralph and Jane, by contrast, comes only after much danger and difficulty.

When Dekker insists in the Epistle, then, that in his play 'nothing is purposed but mirth', he may seem to be doing less than justice to the emotional and tonal range of the comedy. But the disclaimer needs to be seen in the light of contemporary theatrical practice. *The Shoemaker's Holiday* is one of the earliest examples of what is known as 'citizen comedy': plays set in London and dealing with the dominant concerns of metropolitan society – class mobility, sexual intrigue and the pursuit of wealth and status. In his detailed evocation of London's streets, taverns, public buildings and outlying areas, and in his concern with the class implications of the two love-plots, Dekker is partly responding to new trends in dramatic writing of the late 1590s that turned a spotlight on urban existence and were mainly concerned to expose its folly and corruption. It would be wrong, however, to describe *The Shoemaker's Holiday* as a satire, although it contains more abrasive commentary on contemporary manners than has sometimes been recognised. Dekker was more in tune with the bourgeois priorities of his audience than were many of his fellow-dramatists, and his emphasis on 'mirth' seems designed to reassure his readers

(including the authorities, who were suspicious of satire) that his
London comedy has no subversive or critical intent, and that it is to
be enjoyed like a festive occasion, affirming the roots of drama in
holiday celebration and bringing the community together to salute
its great civic traditions.

However, other comic strategies do make an appearance in the
play, and they are occasionally disconcerting. An example can be
found in Scene 2, where Sybil describes for her mistress the meeting
she has just had in town with Rose's lover. After commenting
sardonically on his extravagant attire ('like one of our yellow silk
curtains'), she goes on:

> I stood at our door in Cornhill, looked at him, he at me indeed; spake
> to him, but he not to me, not a word... He passed by me as
> proud – Marry, foh! Are you grown humorous? thought I – and so shut
> the door ...

When Rose protests (in insipid verse) that 'No dove was ever half
so mild as he', Sybil retorts:

> Mild? Yea, as a bushel of stamped crabs! He looked upon me as sour as
> verjuice. Go thy ways, thought I ...   (2.30–9)

Sybil's criticism of Lacy's finery echoes Lincoln's remarks in the
opening scene (lines 12–15), and her description of his behaviour in
London, although it is not corroborated, sounds like a realistic
corrective to Rose's lovesick and partial view. This is partly an
effect of style: Rose's language throughout the play is stilted and
colourless, whilst Sybil's spirited prose creates a deft satirical
sketch. But the question arises as to whether it should (or does)
influence our view of Lacy, and indeed whether it should guide the
manner in which he is presented on stage. Dekker may have felt
tempted to appeal to middle-class priorities in showing Lacy as
initially flashy and unreliable, an aristocratic prodigal who must
earn the right to win his love; but he also seeks to demonstrate the
poverty of judgements based on class. The opening scene contains
an elaborate skirmish between Lincoln and Oatley in which neither
will declare his real motive for opposing the love-match; and when
presented with the information that Lacy was forced to take up
shoemaking on the Continent after squandering his resources,
Oatley reveals the crippling extent of his prejudices:

> As for your nephew, let your lordship's eye
> But watch his action and you need not fear,
> For I have sent my daughter far enough.
> And yet your cousin Roland might do well
> Now he hath learned an occupation.   (1.39–43)

The thinly veiled sneer at courtly indolence also betrays a contempt
for lowly trades that is more openly declared in a later scene by
Oatley's horror when he thinks Rose has eloped with an artisan
(16. 39–45). Ironically, his prediction that shoemaking will solve all
Lacy's problems turns out to be correct, but the play exposes a large
gap between his bourgeois pieties and the joyful energy of Eyre's
shop, where Lacy can 'clothe his cunning with the Gentle Craft'
(3. 4) and turn work into a theatrical device to overcome class
barriers and the vested interests that sustain them.

Lacy's place in the audience's sympathies is not immediately
stabilised by his appearance in disguise: for instance, Firk's
ridiculing of his stage Dutch ('Yaw, yaw – he speaks yawing like a
jackdaw that gapes to be fed with cheese-curds') is an effective
lampoon which initially saddles the play's romantic lead with
another stock part, that of the stage foreigner whose language and
habits are traditionally comic. But while the stereotype confirms
Firk's prejudices, we are forced by our prior knowledge of Lacy's
designs to suspend our conventional response to such a figure and
see his arrival as an interesting breach of the shoemakers' self-
contained world. Furthermore, Lacy's disguise works to his
advantage in the emerging rivalry with Hammon. As critics have
noted, much of the criticism that attaches itself to Lacy in the early
scenes is deflected by Hammon's social posturing in scenes 5 and 6,
playing the country gentleman in the hunt and the courtly lover in
his encounter with Rose: the result in both cases is clumsy and self-
conscious, as he mistakes affectation for style. In his chic
description of the quarry ('The game's not far. / This way with
wingèd feet he fled from death'), and in the lifeless clichés of the
wooing scene, Hammon betrays a false gentility which seems to be
the real target of Simon Eyre's vigorous advice to Rose when he
hears that she is defying her father's wishes:

> Be ruled, sweet Rose. Thou'rt ripe for a man: marry not with a boy
> that has no more hair on his face than thou hast on thy cheeks. A
> courtier? – wash, go by! Stand not upon pishery-pashery. Those silken
> fellows are but painted images – outsides, outsides, Rose; their inner
> linings are torn. No, my fine mouse, marry me with a Gentleman
> Grocer like my Lord Mayor your father.
>
> (11. 37–43)

If we seek a correlative for the speech in the 'images' the play has
given us, we are more likely at this stage to find it in Hammon, who
only two scenes earlier had been courting Rose in his finery, than in
Lacy, disguised as Hans since Scene 4. The irony does not spoil
Eyre's case but rather helps to prove his point that inner worth or
intrinsic nobility is what matters: Lacy's working disguise, like a

romance hero's ordeal, has mended his inner linings, while Hammon's ornate appearance is a poor cover for his spiritual vulgarity.[1] Eyre asserts his bourgeois loyalties in dogmatic fashion, but without Oatley's narrow and calculating snobbery: his speech is less concerned with class distinction as such than with a basic notion of *substance*, to be found not only in the material wealth of a Gentleman Grocer but also in the virile energy which Eyre himself habitually displays and which is conspicuously lacking in the pallid Hammon.

We can see here how Eyre's vitality begins to act as a solvent of class differences, rephrasing the play's conflicts in terms of an opposition between generous spontaneity and rigid self-seeking. This new perspective consistently shows Hammon in an unfavourable light, but in the later scenes it also lends insight into his shortcomings: behind the wealthy bourgeois who tries to buy what he wants, we see an awkward and inhibited young man who is desperate to find a wife and whose emotional incapacity leads him into disastrous misjudgements. When he comes to woo Jane in Scene 12 he is his own worst enemy, as he leads up to his proposal with enquiries about the price of her wares, and botches the crucial moment with a crass disclaimer:

HAMMON   And how this band?
JANE
  Cheap too.
HAMMON   All cheap. How sell you then this hand?
JANE
  My hands are not to be sold.
HAMMON   To be given, then.
  Nay, faith, I come to buy.   (12. 26–9)

That hasty last remark might have half-decent motives behind it (not wanting to rush Jane, or assuring her of his sound standing), but it also betrays Hammon's inclination, behind his sentimental yearning for Jane, to accept the popular myth which identified female shopkeepers with prostitutes. When Jane repudiates this advance, he tries another tack:

HAMMON
  Good sweet, leave work a little while; let's play.
JANE
  I cannot live by keeping holiday.   (lines 30–1)

---

[1] See Michael Manheim, 'The Construction of *The Shoemakers' Holiday*', *Studies in English Literature*, 10 (1970), 315.

The encounter reveals an ugly side to the mercantile prosperity endorsed by Eyre in his remarks to Rose in the previous scene; but it also sets Hammon's illegitimate notions of holiday against the idea of festivity that is alive in the play at large. As R.L. Smallwood points out, Hammon is vulnerable to our judgement because 'in a play filled with scenes of men working, he is always idle';[2] and in the final scenes his own wedding plans are shown to be the outcome of dalliance and deception, and are destroyed by an aggressive holiday spirit ('Cry clubs for prentices!') that derives from solidarity of work and good fellowship. Hammon's humiliation at the hands of the shoemakers is cathartic in effect, clearing the way to the play's resolution, and eliminating from Eyre's holiday kingdom all that is solitary, self-centred and sterile: his last words ('during my life / I vow no woman else shall be my wife') sufficiently indicate why there is no place for him in the final scene. Comedy often requires such a figure (compare Malvolio in *Twelfth Night*); yet this may not prevent us feeling that Hammon is treated with unnecessary harshness, and that the mood of unity at the close depends upon the suppression or exclusion of awkward social realities. It is at this point that we need to consider more closely the figure of Simon Eyre and the ways in which he determines and controls his immediate environment.

As suggested earlier, Eyre's domination of the play-world does not register so much in terms of plot – his conquest of public offices – as in his verbal power and confidence. Nothing in Dekker's sources prepares us for the sound of Eyre's voice, which welds familiar devices and influences – among them the 'huffing' roles of earlier drama, exotic brands of invective, and standard rhetorical devices like alliteration – into a very distinctive idiom, one which reflects the Renaissance obsession with the potentialities of language, its capacity to order and persuade and transform. Despite its colloquial rhythms and salty vocabulary we are always aware that it is an invented speech, which superbly characterises its user but does not represent the language of everyday transactions; and Dekker exploits this gap between language and actuality in his portrayal of Eyre's controlling methods. Early on we are made aware of the limits of his influence, when in the opening scene he comes on full of self-importance, promising to get Ralph discharged since 'I am a man of the best presence' (line 125). But as soon as he sees that his attempt to bribe Lacy and Askew with new boots has failed, he launches a fresh initiative, silencing the protests and pleading of the women:

[2] *The Shoemaker's Holiday*, ed. Smallwood and Wells, p. 36

> Take him, brave men. Hector of Troy was a hackney to him, Hercules
> and Termagant scoundrels. Prince Arthur's Round Table, by the Lord
> of Ludgate, ne'er fed such a tall, such a dapper swordman. By the life
> of Pharaoh, a brave, resolute swordman. Peace, Jane. I say no more,
> mad knaves. (1. 166–71)

What is really a tactical retreat, as Eyre repairs his dignity in the
eyes of his household, is apparently welcomed by the participants in
the scene as an inspiring fiction. This is true at any rate for the men
present: Hodge dispatches Ralph to the wars as eagerly as he earlier
defended his right to stay, and Askew (perhaps with a hint of irony)
implies that Eyre should be congratulated for producing 'so resolute
a soldier' (line 176). If the women do not speak at this point, it is
perhaps because they recognise the futility of opposing this
bombastic endorsement of masculine values. Dekker's audience,
however, is relatively free at this stage to observe Eyre's
manipulation of the scene, and to perceive how his threadbare
catalogue of heroes, from Hector to the Lord of Ludgate, functions
as a kind of pedigree, one that lends shape to the fantasies and
aspirations of the self-made man.

This is not to claim that we can remain uninvolved in Eyre's
rhetoric and still respond to the play. His is too central and
dominant a voice for that. But Dekker is careful to present the
social realities that Eyre's language seeks to master and transform,
and he does not sentimentalise Eyre's authority. The same cannot
always be said for productions of the play: as with Shakespeare's
Falstaff, the stage tradition accumulates mannerisms and stock
approaches; and there has always been a tendency to play Eyre as a
swaggerer with a heart of gold whose trademark is an unflagging
heartiness. This easily becomes tedious, and it obscures much of the
detail of Dekker's portrayal. Take Eyre's attempts to rouse his
household at the start of Scene 4:

> Where be these boys, these girls, these drabs, these scoundrels? They
> wallow in the fat brewis of my bounty, and lick up the crumbs of my
> table, yet will not rise to see my walks cleansed. Come out, you
> powder-beef queans! What, Nan! What, Madge Mumblecrust! Come
> out, you fat midriff-swag-belly whores, and sweep me these kennels,
> that the noisome stench offend not the nose of my neighbours. What,
> Firk, I say! (4. 1–8)

Jonas Barish has suggested that Eyre's language 'is a red herring,
designed to secure an illegitimate sympathy for the character';[3] but
although this speech is often cited as a piece of boisterous fun, we

[3] Jonas A. Barish, Ben Jonson and the Language of Prose Comedy (Cambridge, Mass., 1960), p. 282

are not obliged to have a purely indulgent response to it. A noisy and rumbustious delivery of the lines can actually make Eyre seem rather ineffectual, more interested in the sound of his own voice than getting anything done; and what ought to emerge in performance is that Eyre is an exacting employer who knows how to get results and has developed his own strategies for gaining loyalty and respect. His grumble that the rest of the household live idly off his wealth is obviously belied by the fact that he is rousing them to continue creating that wealth; but we notice that most of Eyre's abuse is reserved for the women of the house, whose work is divided between domestic labour and support services like spinning thread (see lines 36–7). This may be why Eyre sounds jovial rather than coercive to male critics (few women have written about this play), for, as G.K. Hunter puts it, what he speaks 'is an entirely believable version of the comic-aggressive dialect that marks self-conscious male camaraderie in all ages.'[4] Firk on his entry knows exactly how to disarm Eyre, teasing him about his 'bandog and bedlam' machismo and asking whether he has been drinking; and, as we see more clearly in Scene 7, where the men threaten to walk out after a reprimand from Margery (lines 29 ff.), the verbal abuse of women helps to generate a feeling of male solidarity which Eyre, with only a little manipulation, can channel into the productive effort:

> Rip, you chitterling, avaunt! Boy, bid the tapster of the Boar's Head fill me a dozen cans of beer for my journeymen. . . . [*Aside to Boy*] An' the knave fills any more than two he pays for them. . . . . Here, you mad Mesopotamians! Wash your livers with this liquor . . . drink and to work. (7. 71–80)

And the realities of employer-worker relations are softened further by Eyre's egalitarian fiction about the innate nobility of all shoemakers:

> Are not these my brave men, brave shoemakers, all gentlemen of the Gentle Craft? Prince am I none, yet am I nobly born, as being the sole son of a shoemaker. Away, rubbish. (7. 45–8)

In pretending to defend his men against female calumny Eyre reasserts his authority over the entire establishment, and on one level it is the old device of divide-and-rule. But Eyre's rhetoric is a theatrical as well as a social instrument, and even while we are conscious of his manipulations, we experience the flattery and invective in the speeches just quoted as verbal inventiveness which

---

[4] G.K. Hunter, 'Bourgeois Comedy: Shakespeare and Dekker', *Shakespeare and his Contemporaries: Essays in Comparison*, ed. E.A.J. Honigmann (Manchester, 1986), p. 6

gives life to its object, so that his household seems to be energised and made whole rather than subdued by his brilliant tirade.

Neil Rhodes has pointed to a similar process at work in the play's metaphorical structure, showing how readily the language of abuse which Eyre uses to regulate his environment is turned into one of festive celebration. The common element is the pervasive imagery of food: Eyre repeatedly 'transforms people into puddings, sops, and joints of meat,'[5] but this reductive process is inverted at the play's climax, where he lays on a feast for the London apprentices, and Firk enthuses that

> venison pasties walk up and down piping hot like sergeants, beef and brewis comes marching in dry-fats, fritters and pancakes comes trolling in in wheelbarrows, hens and oranges hopping in porters' baskets... (18.195–9)

This fantasy of collaboration in which dishes come to life and hasten to be consumed is a tribute to Eyre's liberality, the social virtue which unlocks all others and makes possible a co-operative, peaceful and well-provided community. The strength of this vision can be gauged from its impact on Firk's language, compelling him to forget his obsessive sexual punning and adopt the fertile, transformative idiom of his master; and it is dramatically satisfying because it concludes a series of official feasts in the play, replacing the hollow rituals of Oatley's regime with a genuine revels. The opening lines of *The Shoemaker's Holiday* are a stiff, perfunctory and probably insincere vote of thanks from Lincoln for one of Oatley's feasts (to which only courtiers have been invited); and later on, when Eyre is entertained by Oatley at Old Ford after his election as sheriff, the shoemaker deals gracefully with his host's clumsy apologies for his 'bad cheer', and proceeds to shake things up with his own vigorous speech, which quite literally acts as a cue for a party –

> What, the Gentle Trade is a living for a man through Europe, through the world!
>
> *A noise within of a tabor and pipe*
>
> (11.46–7)

– and his men enter with a morris dance. In the theatre, of course, such conviviality is irresistible, injecting life into the performance and releasing the audience's holiday instincts; and it installs Eyre as the true author of the occasion. As a result, when Eyre as Lord Mayor stages his own banquet, the democratic vision of the good life offered in Firk's speech is the culmination of a process in which

[5] Neil Rhodes, *Elizabethan Grotesque* (London, 1980), p. 75

the festive occasion has been reclaimed for the whole of society. At the same time it confirms and validates Eyre's power, linking his holiday regime (through the people-as-food metaphor) to his rough-tongued regulation of everyday working life.

The scenes featuring the shoemakers clearly encourage the idea that the holiday established at the end is generated by the ethos Eyre has created in his shop, where high spirits, comradely banter and communal songs already have a festive air about them. This is a very idealised view of labour, though Dekker is careful to give it a solid context in talk about shoemakers' tools and arguments about hiring and firing (see 4. 47 ff., 10. 84–8). We are told nothing about the economics of Eyre's business, and when the question of raising capital arises, in his bid in Scene 7 to buy the ship's cargo, it is Lacy who advances the money and makes all the arrangements. This deal, rather than Eyre's chosen trade, is what paves the way to his future success, but Dekker is careful not to stress the point, preferring to keep up the general impression that, as Alexander Leggatt puts it, 'Simon Eyre became Lord Mayor of London because he was a jolly and energetic shoemaker.'[6] In preserving this legend, with its overtones of Dick Whittington, the play suggests that Eyre's attainment of high office is a proper outcome of his skill and pride in his craft, the pride that makes him feel like a prince and so befits him for public service. Of course, Dekker could have eliminated altogether the ship's cargo episode he found in Deloney and built up a picture of Eyre as a successful businessman; but a materialistic and class-bound figure would contradict everything that is implied by the range and freedom of Eyre's language. Instead, by having him subsidised by aristocratic wealth in the form of Lacy's loan, Dekker creates an alliance across class lines which acts as a rebuke to the petty antagonism of Lincoln and Oatley and plays down the idea of monetary gain in favour of an altogether vaguer notion of social co-operation.

The point is not that Eyre's success actually depends on class alliance, but that his vitality dissolves social barriers and is felt to create the conditions for his own rise to power. Lacy for his part declares that during his time in Eyre's shop he 'lived as merry as an emperor' (21. 144), and at this stage of the play the simile seems entirely appropriate, a recognition that being 'princely born' is a matter not of rank but of capacity, a sense of being empowered by good company and fulfilling work. The play insists on the legitimacy of this conviction, but it is at odds with the social facts, as we expect the play's ending to reveal, and indeed the King himself is afraid

[6] Alexander Leggatt, *Citizen Comedy in the Age of Shakespeare* (Toronto, 1973), p. 19

that his arrival will spoil the festive mood by making Eyre remember his place:

> I am with child till I behold this huffcap.
> But all my doubt is, when we come in presence,
> His madness will be dashed clean out of countenance.
>
> (19. 10–12)

But in the event the King has his own uses for a holiday situation in which social taboos and conventions of behaviour are suspended. In taking charge of affairs in the final scene he is careful not to subdue Eyre's ebullience, and he adopts a playfully theatrical manner to resolve immediate difficulties. Lacy is not only pardoned but given a knighthood, and the latter seems almost to be part of a game the King is playing with Oatley and Lincoln, as he divorces and then reunites the young couple:

> Arise, Sir Roland Lacy. Tell me now,
> Tell me in earnest, Oatley, canst thou chide,
> Seeing thy Rose a lady and a bride?   (21. 114–16)

Romantic expectations are fulfilled, in the formula that 'love respects no blood, / Cares not for difference of birth or state' (21. 104–5), but the King seems more interested in speculating with the intricacies of rank to outwit the opponents of festive renewal. The emphasis is firmly on the energies and fresh possibilities that holiday brings into play. The triumph of young love is part of this process, as it must be in a romantic comedy; yet even on their wedding-day Rose and Lacy cannot compete with Eyre's virile enthusiasm:

> My liege, I am six-and-fifty year old, yet I can cry hump with a sound
> heart for the honour of Saint Hugh. Mark this old wench, my King: I
> danced the shaking of the sheets with her six-and-thirty years ago, and
> yet I hope to get two or three young Lord Mayors ere I die.
>
> (lines 27–31)

And as the stage fills with Eyre's apprentices, his 'true Trojans' (line 147), the King's mind turns to the wars in France:

> With the old troop which there we keep in pay
> We will incorporate a new supply.   (lines 138–9)

Some have seen this as reality breaking in, as it did at the start of the play when war took Ralph from his wife and community, but the King's closing speech hardly acknowledges a gap between duty and pleasure:

Come lords, a while let's revel it at home.
When all our sports and banquetings are done,
Wars must right wrongs which Frenchmen have begun.

(lines 192–4)

The emphasis on virility and male solidarity throughout this scene suggests rather that war is to be the continuation of holiday by other means, revelling abroad rather than at home, perpetuating the happy situation in which, as G.K. Hunter puts it, 'virility and "good heart" will, once again, count for more than money or social success.'[7] As in another play performed in 1599, Shakespeare's *Henry V*, much emphasis is placed on the band of brothers united by common purpose in what the shoemakers call 'incomprehensible good fellowship' (18. 206–7); and it is likely that Dekker's populist monarch was meant to remind his audience of the king whose victory over the French at Agincourt had recently been staged by Shakespeare's company at the rival Globe playhouse.

The identification is not made too precise, though, and the reasons for this may emerge, finally, from a consideration of the play's title. Henry V's great battle was fought on St Crispin's Day, 25 October, a shoemakers' holiday whose foundation is described by Deloney (Part 1, Chapter 9); but in his play Dekker does not mention Agincourt or the festival with which it coincided. The quarto texts of *The Shoemaker's Holiday* have no apostrophe in the title, but most editors have preferred to give the plural form (*Shoemakers'*), influenced perhaps by the communal atmosphere of Eyre's shop and Firk's prompt naming of the holiday they have been granted:

... when the pancake bell rings, we are as free as my Lord Mayor. We may shut up our shops and make holiday. I'll have it called Saint Hugh's Holiday. (18. 209–11)

In his enthusiasm Firk appropriates for the shoemakers (whose patron saint was St Hugh) the Shrovetide holiday which Eyre has declared for '*all* the prentices in London' (line 204). But as L.D. Timms points out, Firk's invention would have put Dekker's audience in mind of 'St Hugh's Day', 17 November, which was the date of Queen Elizabeth's accession to the throne and was by 1599 a major national holiday.[8] In such a context celebration is universal and inclusive, not the prerogative of a single guild, and the echoes of Henry V and St Crispin are held in check by the obvious

[7] Hunter, 'Bourgeois Comedy', p. 8
[8] L.D. Timms, 'Dekker's *The Shoemaker's Holiday* and Elizabeth's Accession Day', *Notes & Queries*, 230 (1985), 58. See also Roy Strong, *The Cult of Elizabeth* (London, 1977), ch. 4.

compliment Dekker pays to his own sovereign in having Eyre promise the King that 'the Gentlemen Shoemakers shall set your sweet Majesty's image cheek by jowl by St Hugh' (21.6–8). The holiday that is Simon Eyre's princely gift to the city, like the building named by the King as Leaden Hall, is offered to Dekker's audience as a tangible link between past and present, affirming the continuity of civic traditions and finding the roots of the great political and economic enterprises of late Elizabethan England in the established rituals of popular culture.

The Play on the Stage

We know from the title-page of the first edition that *The Shoemaker's Holiday* was given at Court in the presence of the Queen on New Year's Day 1600, and this presumably means that it had been a success at the Rose Theatre during the preceding autumn. Although no records have survived of performance on the public stage during Dekker's life, the play was reprinted several times before the closing of the theatres in 1642, and this suggests that it probably enjoyed a number of revivals. Its appeal for citizen audiences of the period is not far to seek. The play is an accessible blend of popular motifs: the rise of the self-made man, the triumph of young love, the celebration of honest labour, and the unifying power of patriotic sentiment; and the affirmation of these things is given weight and depth by Dekker's skilful dramatisation of negative forces opposing them: class division, meanness, poverty, and exploitation. To an Elizabethan audience *The Shoemaker's Holiday* must have provided some of the same pleasures that television soap opera with a middle- or working-class setting does today: a familiar environment, ordinary folk and everyday situations turned into a multiple pattern of incident and climax, with minor heroes and the occasional scapegoat to provide a tactful hint of moral design, flattering and reassuring its audience. And a little later, in the opening decades of the seventeenth century, the play's glorification of civic tradition and stable community may well have satisfied the nostalgia for things Elizabethan that was one response to the tensions and uncertainties of life under the early Stuart kings.

The play continued to be reprinted up to 1657, but it was not judged suitable for the Restoration stage (whose passion for wit did not accommodate rough Elizabethan humour), and it disappeared from the repertory for the next 250 years, until its revival at the very end of the nineteenth century. Since then it has been frequently produced both by amateur groups (with whom the play has been consistently popular), and on the professional stage, with notable productions in the 1920s, including one at the Old Vic with

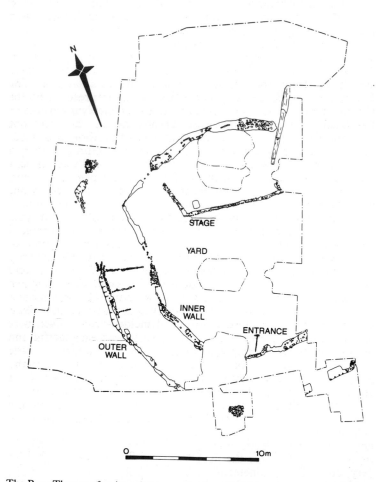

The Rose Theatre after its enlargement in the early 1590s: the drawing shows the partially excavated foundations. (Photo: Andrew Fulgoni © The Museum of London. Reproduced with permission.)

Edith Evans as a memorable Margery, and a major revival in 1981 at the National Theatre, to be considered in a moment.

The original staging of *The Shoemaker's Holiday* is of particular interest because it was first performed at the Rose Theatre in Southwark, whose remains were discovered and partially excavated in 1989.[9] The Rose was a polygonal building originally put up in 1587 and later extended by its owner, Philip Henslowe, to provide more room for spectators and a slightly bigger stage. It was in this enlarged playhouse, capable of holding about 2500 people, that *The Shoemaker's Holiday* received its première. As in the other public theatres of the time, there was a platform stage jutting into the yard, with spectators on three sides of it: in the Rose it tapered slightly towards the front, and was about 18 feet deep, with a total area of 533 square feet. When we compare this with an estimated depth of $10\frac{1}{2}$ feet for the galleries running round the walls and a yard area of about 1700 square feet, it would seem that the stage did not dominate the arena quite as much as has sometimes been supposed; but it was still an open and fluid playing space, unencumbered by a proscenium and affording intimate contact between actors and audience (exploited by Dekker at, for instance, 16. 95–7), and probably permitting entries, particularly of a processional kind, from the yard (see note to 1. 239).

It has been generally assumed that the rear wall of this and other Elizabethan stages consisted of a projecting facade or *frons scenae*, forming the front of the tiring house, with a number of openings: probably a door on either side and a curtained (or double-doored) recess in the middle which could be used for 'discoveries' and storage of properties needed during the action. Such a recess might also contain a booth which could be carried forward to represent a specific location such as a house or shop. Again, however, the Rose excavations prompt a reassessment – as far at least as this particular playhouse is concerned. Nothing has been found to suggest that the front of the tiring house projected into the arena, so that the stage seems rather 'to have been backed by a wall that followed the polygonal line of the main frame', with the tiring house 'fitted out in the bays of the main frame behind the stage'. Interestingly, excavation revealed the brick foundations of this wall (in the enlarged theatre) to be curved rather than angled; although, since

[9] See John Orrell and Andrew Gurr, 'What the Rose can tell us', *Times Literary Supplement*, 9–15 June 1989, pp. 636, 649, for a preliminary analysis of the dig; a fuller investigation, with more accurate measurements, has been made by Julian Bowsher and Simon Blatherwick in 'The Structure of the Rose', contributed to a recent conference on 'New Issues in the Reconstruction of Shakespeare's Theatre', proceedings to be edited by Franklin J. Hildy (University of Georgia Press, forthcoming).

Elizabethan carpenters lacked the knowledge to bend timbers, the significance of this for the superstructure is unclear.[10]

All this suggests that the design of the Rose stage was even more simply functional than previously imagined. The rear of the stage becomes a sequence of angled segments, which does not disallow the idea of a 'central' discovery space but probably means that it was the same size as the doorways; and the number of the latter may have been determined not by symmetry but simply by the number of segments adjoining the stage area. This may help to explain the stage direction at the start of Scene 12: '*Enter* JANE *in a sempster's shop . . . and* HAMMON . . . *at another door.*' As Stanley Wells points out,[11] if only two doors were used for entries we would expect the direction to read 'at the other door', unless we assume that Jane is 'discovered' at work in a centre recess and steps forward to play the scene, with Hammon entering at one of the doors on either side. But the evidence from the Rose site, fragmentary as it is, suggests that theories about discovery spaces, not to mention booths or stalls, should be treated with caution. If the tiring house was confined within the rear bays of the main frame, there would have been little room for large structures or for group tableaux like the one suggested at the start of Scene 13: '*Enter* HODGE *at his shop board*, RALPH, FIRK, LACY *and a Boy, at work.*' While a discovery is not impossible here, it seems more likely that the characters come in through one or more doors, singing and carrying stools and equipment, and simply get on with the scene. (This, or something like it, is what most modern companies not using a proscenium stage would do.) Stanley Wells[12] has made the attractive suggestion that directions like 'at his shop board' and Eyre's command 'Open my shop windows' (4.8–9) were fulfilled by having one or more of the stage doors fitted with shutters which let down to form shop counters: given the frequency of shop scenes in the drama of this period such a device might have become a shorthand convention obviating the need for elaborate settings to indicate location.

Whatever the precise details of Elizabethan staging, it is important to stress its economy and fluency. Dekker's theatre was probably faster-paced than ours and managed transitions and shifts of location with the minimum of interruption, so it is important to be clear about how the action is divided up. This edition, like others before it, abandons the act divisions imposed on the text in the last century and divides the action into scenes (see Note on the Text below); but while this comes closer to identifying Dekker's basic

---

[10] Orrell and Gurr, p. 636
[11] Smallwood and Wells, pp. 44–5
[12] Smallwood and Wells, p. 46

design it can still be misleading. For instance, at the end of Scene 13 the shoemakers decide to have breakfast and leave the stage, and the next scene brings in Hammon's servant looking for Eyre's shop. His call attracts Ralph, whose bemusement at being presented with Jane's shoe means that he forgets about eating (14. 38). Clearly the action is continuous, with Ralph re-entering almost immediately, and one is tempted to remove the scene division. But the entire movement of the play depends upon this sort of unobtrusive punctuation, with the stage being cleared between blocks of dramatic action which play off against one another – in this case, juxtaposing Hans/Lacy's summons to fit Rose's shoes (13. 54–5) with the echoing Cinderella motif of Ralph rediscovering his wife; and setting Eyre's imminent success at the expense of the dead aldermen (13. 35–9) against Ralph's hopes for a change in his fortunes. As this last example shows, Dekker also uses this technique to solve the problem of varying time-schemes in the separate storylines: Eyre's swift promotion seems less implausible when it is flanked by love plots moving rapidly to a climax. But if Dekker thinks in scenic units, he also makes dramatic narrative out of their interaction, and for this a flexible, unencumbered stagecraft is essential.

The twentieth century has confirmed the play's stageworthiness, and for a long time it was the most popular non-Shakespearean comedy of its period. Even so, its theatrical fortunes have been mixed. Early revivals by university and other groups interested in staging long-neglected plays eventually led to two major pro-ductions in 1922 and 1926, both of which were well received; and subsequently it was directed in an adapted version by Orson Welles (1938) and was produced for radio in 1958 by Donald Wolfit as Simon Eyre. There have been many other productions, but it is clear from the excellent survey by Stanley Wells of the play's stage history[13] that in many of these, as he puts it, 'directors have betrayed unease and distrust either of the play or of their audiences' possible reactions. Apparently embarrassed by the play's emotional directness, they have laboured too hard to sophisticate it with comic and interpretative business.' He cites numerous reviews and concludes that the play 'offers ample scope for idiosyncratic character acting, but detail must not overwhelm the design; the commonest complaints have been of over-fussiness, excessive heartiness, and caricature'.[14]

In recent years the professional stage has been more adventurous

---

[13] Smallwood and Wells, pp. 44–53. See also Lisa Cronin, *Checklist of Professional Productions ... since 1880, Renaissance Drama Newsletter*, Supplement Seven (1987), pp. 15–18

[14] Smallwood and Wells, pp. 52–3

in exploring the Elizabethan repertory, and *The Shoemaker's Holiday* has been correspondingly less in demand. In 1978 Nat Brenner directed his Old Vic students in a production at the Theatre Royal, Bristol; and in 1981 the play finally reached the National Theatre in John Dexter's production with Alfred Lynch as Eyre and Brenda Bruce as Margery. Dexter made effective use of the large Olivier stage, breaking it up with arches which helped to localise the different settings (particularly Eyre's shop), and using tapestries drawn across the back with views of the Royal Exchange, St Paul's, and a hunting scene. The production received generally favourable reviews and encouraged some thoughtful reassessment of the play's merits. However, a surprising number of critics found it sprawling, loosely constructed, even badly plotted, possibly as a consequence of Dexter's copiously detailed evocation of Elizabethan domestic and working life, in which bells rang, chamberpots were emptied, rushes strewn, pipes lit, beer consumed – processes which some felt overloaded the play and made it difficult to follow. Others saw this kind of detail as bringing out the material urban realities of characters' lives, the economic facts underlying the romantic, sentimental and idealised story lines.

What seems to be at issue here is the nature of the comedy: one critic wanted to see it as 'a sort of Elizabethan Arnold Wesker analysis of a society at work'[15] (and so reinforcing its links with more satirical citizen comedy); but some took the view that Dexter was working against the grain of the play in emphasising the realistic elements. A prime example is Ralph's return from the wars in Scene 10, a very effective moment in Dexter's production (see note to 10.57). Benedict Nightingale, who in his *New Statesman* review pointed to the general problem of reconciling 'socio-historical truths with rags to riches fantasy and fun', objected to the emphasis given to Ralph's injury and in particular to the way his sudden appearance 'visibly infects with guilt the lovelorn nob Lacy'[16] (who sent Ralph to the wars whilst evading them himself). Lacy's reaction was perhaps a dubious piece of underlining, but it raises the question of what is happening when we interpret an old text in terms of modern values and assumptions. By playing up the irony of Ralph's misfortune did the production read into Lacy an inappropriate liberal guilt? Or was it a legitimate gloss on the play's portrayal of class differences? Again, Ralph's entry undeniably alters the mood of the scene, causing surprise, shock and embarrassment; but is Margery's joke at his expense ("Twas a fair gift of God the infirmity took not hold a little higher') a piece of

---

[15] Peter Conrad, 'Critics' Forum', BBC broadcast, 27 June 1981
[16] Benedict Nightingale, review in *New Statesman*, 26 June 1981

tactless stupidity or evidence of an unsqueamish Elizabethan capacity to deal with unavoidable suffering by laughing at it? Would Dekker's audience have agreed that Margery's catch-phrase 'but let that pass' is 'for once, supremely appropriate' (as R.L. Smallwood argues in a fine analysis[17]), or regarded her comic idiom as the best therapy available?

Margery, as played by Brenda Bruce, was in some respects the dominant character in Dexter's production. It was she rather than Eyre who emerged as larger than life, disporting herself in the later scenes (as Michael Coveney put it in the *Financial Times*) 'in the gaudy apparel of the Virgin Queen gone wrong'.[18] Alfred Lynch avoided making Eyre rumbustious, and according to John Wilders 'gave a sense of grittiness, of a man who has worked very hard to get to the top and has had disappointments on the way'.[19] Critics divided as to the effectiveness of this reading of the part (some thought that it lacked the necessary energy), but it avoided the clichés of past performances. Another unexpected and very entertaining performance came from David Yelland as the King. Played as a suave parody of Olivier's Henry V, 'dubbing knights as casually as one might flick the ash off a cigarette',[20] this was a theatrical sovereign (matching Eyre's holiday monarch) whose next stop was clearly destined to be the denouement of another play.

A NOTE ON THE TEXT

The text of the present edition is based on a copy of the first quarto of 1600 (Q1) in the British Library, and checked against the text and collations in the Revels edition of the play by R.L. Smallwood and Stanley Wells (Manchester 1979). Q1 is a black-letter text which seems to have been printed from Dekker's manuscript, judging by some rather vague stage directions (e.g., at the start of Scene 18) and inconsistent speech prefixes. Such things would have been tidied up in a promptbook version and cues established for the three-man songs, which as things stand cannot be assigned a definite place in the action and so are here printed after Dekker's Epistle and Prologue. (It seems likely that they were late additions to the play.)

Spelling and punctuation have been modernised, but the pseudo-Dutch speeches of Hans/Lacy are preserved in their original form

[17] Smallwood and Wells, p. 31
[18] Michael Coveney, review in *Financial Times*, 22 June 1981
[19] John Wilders, 'Kaleidoscope', BBC broadcast, 23 June 1981
[20] Ian Stewart, review in *Country Life*, 9 July 1981

except for minor spelling changes to make them more consistent and intelligible. In speech prefixes and stage directions titles like 'Lord Mayor' and 'Eyre's wife' in Q1 have been replaced by the character's name; and a single form is adopted for those (Lacy, Hodge) who are identified by more than one name. Stage directions that do not originate in Q1 are placed in square – as opposed to round – brackets; other departures from Q1 (unless they correct obvious misprints) are recorded in the collation. I have used the form *An'* wherever Q1 has *And* in its obsolete sense of 'if'. Finally, Q1 has no act or scene divisions, and the arrangement offered here of twenty-one scenes (the same as that adopted by Smallwood and Wells in their Revels edition) simply reflects the fact that the stage is cleared twenty times in the course of the action. Dekker did not think in terms of a five-act structure when composing his play.

FURTHER READING

Editions

R.L. Smallwood and Stanley Wells, *The Shoemaker's Holiday*. The Revels Plays. Manchester, 1979. Modernised text with full commentary and critical introduction; much the best modern edition

Fredson Bowers, *The Dramatic Works of Thomas Dekker*. Vol. I, Cambridge 1953. Original spelling text; principally of use to specialists, but valuably supplemented by:

Cyrus Hoy, *Introductions, Notes, and Commentaries to texts in 'The Dramatic Works of Thomas Dekker'*. Vol. I, Cambridge, 1980

Paul C. Davies, *The Shoemakers' Holiday*. Edinburgh, 1968. Original spelling text with light commentary and short introduction

Merritt E. Lawlis, *The Novels of Thomas Deloney*. Bloomington, Indiana, 1961

E.D. Pendry, *Thomas Dekker: Selected Writings*. Stratford-upon-Avon Library, 4, London, 1967 (non-dramatic works)

Books

James H. Conover, *Thomas Dekker: An Analysis of Domestic Structure*. The Hague, 1969

M.-T. Jones-Davies, *Un Peintre de la Vie Londonienne: Thomas Dekker*. 2 vols. Paris, 1958

Alexander Leggatt, *Citizen Comedy in the Age of Shakespeare*. Toronto, 1973

G.R. Price, *Thomas Dekker*. New York, 1969

Articles

Arthur Brown, 'Citizen Comedy and Domestic Drama', *Jacobean Theatre*, ed. J.R. Brown and B. Harris. Stratford-upon-Avon Studies I, London, 1960

Julia Gasper, 'Dekker's Word-Play in *The Shoemakers' Holiday*', *Notes & Queries*, 230 (1985), 58-9

George K. Hunter, 'Bourgeois Comedy: Shakespeare and Dekker', *Shakespeare and his Contemporaries: Essays in Comparison*, ed. E.A.J. Honigmann. Manchester, 1986

Joel H. Kaplan, 'Virtue's Holiday: Thomas Dekker and Simon Eyre', *Renaissance Drama*, New Series 2 (1969), 103-22

Arthur F. Kinney, 'Thomas Dekker's Twelfth Night', *University of Toronto Quarterly*, 41 (1971), 63-73

Michael Manheim, 'The Construction of *The Shoemakers' Holiday*', *Studies in English Literature*, 10 (1970), 315

Peter Mortenson, 'The Economics of Joy in *The Shoemakers' Holiday*', *Studies in English Literature*, 16 (1976), 241–52

L.D. Timms, 'Dekker's *The Shoemaker's Holiday* and Elizabeth's Accession Day', *Notes & Queries*, 230 (1985), 58

ABBREVIATIONS

ed.	an editor
NT	National Theatre
Q1	First Quarto of 1600
sd	stage direction
sp	speech prefix

THE
SHOMAKERS
Holiday.
OR
The Gentle Craft.

With the humorous life of Simon
Eyre, ſhoomaker, and Lord Maior
of London.

As it was acted before the Queenes moſt excellent Ma-
ieſtie on New-yeares day at night laſt, by the right
honourable the Earle of Notingham, Lord high Ad-
mirall of England, his ſeruants.

Printed by Valentine Sims dwelling at the foote of Adling
hill, neere Bainards Caſtle, at the ſigne of the White
Swanne, and are there to be ſold.
1 6 0 0.

THE
SHOMAKERS
Holiday,
OR
The Gentle Craft.

With the humorous life of Simon
Eyre, Shoemaker, and Lord Maior
of London.

As it was acted before the Queenes most excellent Ma-
iestie on New-yeares day at night last, by the right
honourable the Earle of Notingham, Lord high Ad-
mirall of England, his seruants.

Printed by Valentine Sims dwelling at the foot of Adling
hill, neere Bainards Castle, at the signe of the White
Swanne, and are there to be sold.
1610.

TO ALL GOOD FELLOWS, PROFESSORS OF THE GENTLE CRAFT, OF WHAT DEGREE SOEVER

Kind gentlemen and honest boon companions, I present you
here with a merry conceited comedy called *The Shoemaker's
Holiday*, acted by my Lord Admiral's Players this present
Christmas before the Queen's most excellent Majesty; for the
mirth and pleasant matter by her Highness graciously   5
accepted, being indeed no way offensive. The argument of the
play I will set down in this epistle: Sir Hugh Lacy, Earl of
Lincoln, had a young gentleman of his own name, his near
kinsman, that loved the Lord Mayor's daughter of London; to
prevent and cross which love, the Earl caused his kinsman to   10
be sent colonel of a company into France, who resigned his
place to another gentleman his friend, and came disguised like
a Dutch shoemaker to the house of Simon Eyre in Tower
Street, who served the Mayor and his household with shoes:
the merriments that passed in Eyre's house, his coming to be   15
Mayor of London, Lacy's getting his love, and other
accidents; with two merry three-man's songs. Take all in good
worth that is well intended, for nothing is purposed but mirth.
Mirth lengtheneth long life, which with all other blessings I
heartily wish you.   20

Farewell.

professors members of the profession
the Gentle Craft then a standard name for the shoemaking trade. Cf. later
assertions that shoemakers are 'nobly born'.
2 *conceited* ingeniously contrived
3 *my Lord Admiral's Players* the principal rival to Shakespeare's company, the
Chamberlain's Men
6 *argument* outline of the plot
17 *accidents* incidents, events
three-man's songs songs for three male voices

[DRAMATIS PERSONAE

THE KING OF ENGLAND
SIR HUGH LACY, EARL OF LINCOLN
ROLAND LACY, *Lincoln's nephew; afterwards disguised as* HANS
  MEULTER
ASKEW, *Lacy's cousin*
CORNWALL
LOVELL
DODGER, *servant to Lincoln*
SIR ROGER OATLEY, *Lord Mayor of London*
ROSE, *Oatley's daughter*
SYBIL, *Rose's maid*
HAMMON, *a city gentleman*
WARNER, *Hammon's brother-in-law*
SCOTT, *a friend of Oatley's*
SIMON EYRE, *shoemaker and afterwards Lord Mayor*
MARGERY, *Eyre's wife*
HODGE (*nickname of* ROGER), *Eyre's foreman*
RALPH DAMPORT, *a journeyman of Eyre's*
JANE, *Ralph's wife*
FIRK, *a journeyman of Eyre's*
A Dutch Skipper
A Boy, *working for Eyre*
A Boy, *with the hunters*
Noblemen, Soldiers, Huntsmen, Shoemakers, Apprentices,
  Servants]

4

THE PROLOGUE

as it was pronounced before the Queen's Majesty

As wretches in a storm, expecting day,
With trembling hands and eyes cast up to heaven
Make prayers the anchor of their conquered hopes,
So we, dear goddess, wonder of all eyes,
Your meanest vassals, through mistrust and fear   5
To sink into the bottom of disgrace
By our imperfect pastimes, prostrate thus
On bended knees our sails of hope do strike,
Dreading the bitter storms of your dislike.

Since, then, unhappy men, our hap is such   10
That to ourselves ourselves no help can bring,
But needs must perish if your saint-like ears,
Locking the temple where all mercy sits,
Refuse the tribute of our begging tongues:
O grant, bright mirror of true chastity,   15
From those life-breathing stars your sun-like eyes
One gracious smile; for your celestial breath
Must send us life, or sentence us to death.

Written for the performance at Court on New Year's Day, 1600
5 *vassals* The pun on 'vessels' sustains the metaphor of a ship at sea. The plural
may imply that the whole cast knelt on stage (see line 8) while one actor spoke
the lines; in modern performance it is common to break up speeches like this
one between several players.
8 *strike* lower

THE FIRST THREE-MAN'S SONG

O the month of May, the merry month of May,
  So frolic, so gay, and so green, so green, so green;
O and then did I unto my true love say,
  Sweet Peg, thou shalt be my summer's queen.

Now the nightingale, the pretty nightingale,   5
  The sweetest singer in all the forest's choir,
Entreats thee, sweet Peggy, to hear thy true love's tale –
  Lo, yonder she sitteth, her breast against a briar.

But O, I spy the cuckoo, the cuckoo, the cuckoo;
  See where she sitteth – come away, my joy.   10
Come away, I prithee, I do not like the cuckoo
  Should sing where my Peggy and I kiss and toy.

O the month of May, the merry month of May,
  So frolic, so gay, and so green, so green, so green;
And then did I unto my true love say,   15
  Sweet Peg, thou shalt be my summer's queen.

The position of the songs in the action is not specified (see Note on the Text);
but the first might be sung in Scene 11 in conjunction with the morris dance at
line 51 (see note). Its mention of the cuckoo, symbol of cuckoldry, anticipates
the threat to Ralph posed by Hammon's pursuit of Jane in the following scene.
 8 *breast . . . briar* The sweet song of the nightingale was supposed to be caused by
the pain of a thorn in her side.

THE SECOND THREE-MAN'S SONG

This is to be sung at the latter end

Cold's the wind, and wet's the rain,
    Saint Hugh be our good speed.
Ill is the weather that bringeth no gain,
    Nor helps good hearts in need.

Troll the bowl, the jolly nut-brown bowl,   5
    And here, kind mate, to thee.
Let's sing a dirge for Saint Hugh's soul,
    And down it merrily.

Down-a-down, hey down-a-down,
    Hey-derry-derry, down-a-down,   10
                (Close with the tenor boy)
Ho, well done, to me let come,
    Ring compass, gentle joy.

Troll the bowl, the nut-brown bowl,
    And here, kind *etc.* (*as often as there be men to drink*)

At last when all have drunk, this verse:

Cold's the wind, and wet's the rain,   15
    Saint Hugh be our good speed.
Ill is the weather that bringeth no gain,
    Nor helps good hearts in need.

Lines 10–11 are similar to the opening of Scene 13, but probably the instruction about 'the latter end' should be taken literally: coming at the very end of the play, the song recalls the audience to the everyday world in a manner reminiscent of Feste's song at the end of Shakespeare's *Twelfth Night*.

5 *Troll* pass
    nut-brown i.e., the colour of the ale it contains
12 *Ring compass, gentle joy* let joy be unconfined

7

THE SHOEMAKER'S HOLIDAY

A pleasant comedy of the Gentle Craft

[Scene 1]

Enter OATLEY *and* LINCOLN

LINCOLN
My Lord Mayor, you have sundry times
Feasted myself and many courtiers more;
Seldom or never can we be so kind
To make requital of your courtesy.
But leaving this, I hear my cousin Lacy   5
Is much affected to your daughter Rose.
OATLEY
True, my good lord; and she loves him so well
That I mislike her boldness in the chase.
LINCOLN
Why, my Lord Mayor, think you it then a shame
To join a Lacy with an Oatley's name?   10
OATLEY
Too mean is my poor girl for his high birth. ⎤ *class &*
Poor citizens must not with courtiers wed,   ⎦ *marriage*
Who will in silks and gay apparel spend
More in one year than I am worth by far.
Therefore your honour need not doubt my girl.   15
LINCOLN
Take heed, my lord, advise you what you do.
A verier unthrift lives not in the world
Than is my cousin; for, I'll tell you what,
'Tis now almost a year since he requested
To travel countries for experience.   20

---

0 sd OATLEY Dekker found the name in Stow's *Survey of London*, where '*Robert
   Oteley*, Grocer' is listed as Lord Mayor in 1434. For the spelling, see the pun at
   Scene 13.31.
1 *sundry* several
5 *cousin* Used more loosely than today (cf. *coz* in line 27 below); Lacy is his
   nephew.
6 *much affected to* besotted with
15 *doubt* worry about

9

I furnished him with coin, bills of exchange,
Letters of credit, men to wait on him,
Solicited my friends in Italy
Well to respect him. But to see the end:
Scant had he journeyed through half Germany   25
But all his coin was spent, his men cast off,
His bills embezzled, and my jolly coz,
Ashamed to show his bankrupt presence here,
Became a shoemaker in Wittenberg –
A goodly science for a gentleman   30
Of such descent! Now judge the rest by this:
Suppose your daughter have a thousand pound,
He did consume me more in one half-year;
And make him heir to all the wealth you have,
One twelve-month's rioting will waste it all.   35
Then seek, my lord, some honest citizen
To wed your daughter to.
OATLEY   I thank your lordship.
    [*Aside*] Well, fox, I understand your subtlety. –
As for your nephew, let your lordship's eye
But watch his actions and you need not fear,   40
For I have sent my daughter far enough.
And yet your cousin Roland might do well
Now he hath learned an occupation.
    [*Aside*] And yet I scorn to call him son-in-law.
LINCOLN
Ay, but I have a better trade for him.   45
I thank his Grace, he hath appointed him
Chief colonel of all those companies
Mustered in London and the shires about
To serve his Highness in those wars of France.

Enter LOVELL, LACY *and* ASKEW

See where he comes. – Lovell, what news with you?   50

41 *sent* ed. (omitted Q1)
49 sd (*after* 50, Q1)

---

21 *bills of exchange* promissory notes
25 *Scant* scarcely
27 *embezzled* wasted
33 *me* i.e., at my expense (a so-called dative form, giving emphasis)
35 *rioting* riotous living
46 *his Grace* i.e., the King

LOVELL
  My Lord of Lincoln, 'tis his Highness' will
  That presently your cousin ship for France
  With all his powers. He would not for a million
  But they should land at Dieppe within four days.
LINCOLN
  Go certify his Grace it shall be done.   55

                           Exit LOVELL
  Now, cousin Lacy, in what forwardness
  Are all your companies?
LACY   All well prepared.
  The men of Hertfordshire lie at Mile End,
  Suffolk and Essex train in Tothill Fields;
  The Londoners and those of Middlesex,   60
  All gallantly prepared in Finsbury,
  With frolic spirits long for their parting hour.
OATLEY
  They have their imprest, coats and furniture,
  And if it please your cousin Lacy come
  To the Guildhall he shall receive his pay,   65
  And twenty pounds besides my brethren
  Will freely give him to approve our loves
  We bear unto my lord your uncle here.
LACY
  I thank your honour.
LINCOLN   Thanks, my good Lord Mayor.
OATLEY
  At the Guildhall we will expect your coming.   *Exit* 70
LINCOLN
  To approve your loves to me? No, subtlety!
  Nephew, that twenty pound he doth bestow
  For joy to rid you from his daughter Rose.
  But, cousins both, now here are none but friends,
  I would not have you cast an amorous eye   75

54 *Dieppe* (Deepe Q1)

---

52 *presently* without delay
53 *powers* forces
56 *forwardness* readiness
58 *Mile End* common ground to the north-east of London used as a military
    training and mustering centre
59 *Tothill Fields* another mustering area in Westminster
61 *Finsbury* fields to the north of the city used for archery practice
63 *imprest* recruitment pay
   furniture equipment   67 *approve* demonstrate

Upon so mean a project as the love
Of a gay, wanton, painted citizen. *Rose*
I know this churl even in the height of scorn
Doth hate the mixture of his blood with thine:
I pray thee, do thou so. Remember, coz,   80
What honourable fortunes wait on thee.
Increase the King's love which so brightly shines *the real source*
And gilds thy hopes; I have no heir but thee –
And yet not thee, if with a wayward spirit
Thou start from the true bias of my love.   85
LACY
My lord, I will for honour – not desire
Of land or livings, or to be your heir –
So guide my actions in pursuit of France
As shall add glory to the Lacys' name.
LINCOLN
Coz, for those words here's thirty portagues;   90
And nephew Askew, there's a few for you.
Fair honour in her loftiest eminence
Stays in France for you till you fetch her thence.
Then, nephews, clap swift wings on your designs.
Begone, begone, make haste to the Guildhall.   95
There presently I'll meet you. Do not stay:
Where honour beckons, shame attends delay.   *Exit*
ASKEW
How gladly would your uncle have you gone!
LACY
True, coz; but I'll o'er-reach his policies.
I have some serious business for three days,   100
Which nothing but my presence can dispatch.
You therefore, cousin, with the companies,
Shall haste to Dover. There I'll meet with you,
Or if I stay past my prefixèd time,
Away for France; we'll meet in Normandy.   105
The twenty pounds my Lord Mayor gives to me
You shall receive, and these ten portagues,
Part of mine uncle's thirty. Gentle coz,

97 *beckons* ed. (becomes Q1)

77 *painted* made up. A standard prejudice against cosmetics is combined with scorn
   at citizen pretensions.
85 *start . . . bias* deviate from the proper course (an image from bowls)
90 *portagues* Portuguese gold coins worth about £5, a considerable sum then
99 *o'er-reach his policies* out-scheme him

Have care to our great charge. I know your wisdom
Hath tried itself in higher consequence.　　　　　110
ASKEW
　Coz, all myself am yours. Yet have this care,
　To lodge in London with all secrecy.
　Our uncle Lincoln hath, besides his own,
　Many a jealous eye that in your face
　Stares only to watch means for your disgrace.　　110

Enter SIMON EYRE, MARGERY, HODGE, FIRK, JANE,
and RALPH *with a piece*

LACY
　Stay, cousin – who be these?
EYRE
　Leave whining, leave whining: away with this whimpering,
　this puling, these blubbering tears, and these wet eyes. I'll
　get thy husband discharged, I warrant thee, sweet Jane – go
　to!　　　　　120
HODGE
　Master, here be the captains.
EYRE
　Peace, Hodge; husht, ye knave, husht.
FIRK
　Here be the cavaliers and the colonels, master.
EYRE
　Peace, Firk; peace, my fine Firk. Stand by, with your
　pishery-pashery, away! I am a man of the best presence: I'll　125
　speak to them an' they were popes! Gentlemen, captains,
　colonels, commanders; brave men, brave leaders, may it

115 sd (*after* 116, Q1)
126 *an'* ed. (and Q1, *passim*)

---

109 *charge* commission
110 *tried ... consequence* been tested in more crucial situations
114 *jealous* vigilant. Lincoln's servants act as his spies.
115 sd *piece* firearm, indicating Ralph's conscription into the army. A cobbler's
　　patch was also often called a *piece*, but it is Ralph's new occupation that is
　　visualised here.
118 *puling* whining
123 *cavaliers* horse soldiers
125 *of* fit for
126 *an'* even if (contraction of *and*)

please you to give me audience. I am Simon Eyre, the mad
shoemaker of Tower Street. This wench with the mealy
mouth that will never tire is my wife, I can tell you. Here's 130
Hodge, my man and my foreman. Here's Firk, my fine firking
journeyman; and this is blubbered Jane. All we come to be
suitors for this honest Ralph. Keep him at home and, as I am a
true shoemaker and a gentleman of the Gentle Craft, buy
spurs yourself and I'll find ye boots these seven years. 135

MARGERY
Seven years, husband?

EYRE
Peace, midriff, peace; I know what I do. Peace!

FIRK
Truly, Master Cormorant, you shall do God good service to
let Ralph and his wife stay together. She's a young, new-
married woman. If you take her husband away from her a- 140
night, you undo her; she may beg in the daytime; for he's as
good a workman at a prick and an awl as any is in our trade.

JANE
O let him stay, else I shall be undone!

FIRK
Ay, truly, she shall be laid at one side like a pair of old shoes
else, and be occupied for no use. 145

LACY
Truly, my friends, it lies not in my power.
The Londoners are pressed, paid and set forth
By the Lord Mayor. I cannot change a man.

HODGE
Why, then you were as good be a corporal as a colonel, if
you cannot discharge one good fellow. And I tell you true, I 150
think you do more than you can answer, to press a man
within a year and a day of his marriage.

140–1 *a-night* ed. (a night Q1)

---

128 *mad* madcap, carefree, exuberant
131 *firking* a bawdy euphemism, as in much of the sport with Firk's name in the
play. More generally the word suggests the character's energy and sense of
mischief.
132 *journeyman* a craftsman who has served his apprenticeship
133 *Ralph* spelled 'Rafe' in Q1, and so pronounced. Cf. the pun in lines 172–3.
138 *Cormorant* corruption of 'coronel', a common Elizabethan spelling (used at line
123 in Q1) of 'colonel'
142 *awl* bawdy pun on 'hole'. Firk takes Jane's *undone* in the next line as another
sexual quibble, and caps it with one of his own (*occupied*) in line 145.
147 *pressed* conscripted

EYRE

Well said, melancholy Hodge! Gramercy, my fine foreman!

MARGERY

Truly, gentlemen, it were ill done for such as you to stand
so stiffly against a poor young wife, considering her case;   155
she is new-married – but let that pass. I pray, deal not
roughly with her. Her husband is a young man and but
newly entered – but let that pass.

EYRE

Away with your pishery-pashery, your pols and your
edepols. Peace, midriff; silence, Cecily Bumtrinket. Let   160
your head speak.

FIRK

Yea, and the horns too, master.

EYRE

Tawsoone, my fine Firk, tawsoone! Peace, scoundrels. See
you this man, captains? You will not release him? Well, let
him go. He's a proper shot: let him vanish! Peace, Jane, dry   165
up thy tears, they'll make his powder dankish. Take him,
brave men. Hector of Troy was a hackney to him, Hercules
and Termagant scoundrels. Prince Arthur's Round Table,
by the Lord of Ludgate, ne'er fed such a tall, such a dapper
swordman. By the life of Pharaoh, a brave, resolute   170
swordman. Peace, Jane; I say no more, mad knaves.

FIRK

See, see, Hodge, how my master raves in commendation of
Ralph.

---

160   *midriff* ed. (Midasse Q1)
163   *Tawsoone* ed. (Too soone Q1)

---

153   *melancholy* wise, thoughtful
154–5   *stand ... against* behave so inflexibly towards. But Margery is unable to avoid
　　　 sexual innuendo, as her catchphrase *but let that pass* frequently acknowledges.
159–60   *pols ... edepols* pleadings and protestations; pointless chatter
160   *Cecily Bumtrinket* later identified as Margery's maid (Scene 4.34–5), and so
　　　 perhaps present here and about to intervene; the character has appeared in
　　　 several productions. But Eyre seems to be using it as a nickname for Margery.
161   *your head* Eyre himself, head of the household
162   *horns* i.e., of cuckoldry – a hackneyed joke
163   *Tawsoone* be quiet (Welsh)
168   *Termagant* god of the Saracens in romance literature and the medieval mystery
　　　 plays, where he is loud and violent
169   *Lord of Ludgate* probably King Lud, legendary founder of London, whose
　　　 statue stood on the east side of Ludgate

HODGE
Ralph, thou'rt a gull, by this hand, an' thou goest not.
ASKEW
I am glad, good master Eyre, it is my hap   175
To meet so resolute a soldier.
Trust me, for your report and love to him
A common, slight regard shall not respect him.
LACY
Is thy name Ralph?
RALPH   Yes, sir.
LACY   Give me thy hand.
Thou shalt not want, as I am a gentleman.   180
Woman, be patient; God no doubt will send
Thy husband safe again, but he must go:
His country's quarrel says it shall be so.
HODGE
Thou'rt a gull, by my stirrup, if thou dost not go! I will not
have thee strike thy gimlet into these weak vessels – prick   185
thine enemies, Ralph.

Enter DODGER

DODGER
My lord, your uncle on the Tower Hill
Stays with the Lord Mayor and the aldermen,
And doth request you with all speed you may
To hasten thither.
ASKEW   Cousin, let's go.   190
LACY
Dodger, run you before. Tell them we come.
                                        Exit DODGER
This Dodger is mine uncle's parasite,
The arrant'st varlet that e'er breathed on earth.
He sets more discord in a noble house

174 *not* ed. (omitted Q1)
191 sd (*after* 190 'thither', Q1)

---

174 *gull* fool
177 *for* because of
178 *A . . . him* he will get more consideration than is usually due to ordinary recruits.
184 *stirrup* shoemaker's strap
185 *weak vessels* women (see I Peter 3.7). The sexual joking continues.
192 *parasite* servant; but the term creates expectations of an artful, scheming
    character like Mosca in Jonson's *Volpone* which Dodger does not fulfil, though
    he may be one of the spies referred to in line 114. In the 1981 NT production
    Dodger lived up to his name by his inability to walk in a straight line.
193 *arrant'st varlet* most unmitigated rascal

By one day's broaching of his pickthank tales   195
Than can be salved again in twenty years;
And he I fear shall go with us to France
To pry into our actions.
ASKEW   Therefore, coz,
It shall behove you to be circumspect.
LACY
Fear not, good cousin. Ralph, hie to your colours.   200
                    [*Exeunt* LACY *and* ASKEW]
RALPH
I must, because there is no remedy.
But, gentle master and my loving dame,
As you have always been a friend to me,
So in mine absence think upon my wife.
JANE
Alas, my Ralph.
MARGERY   She cannot speak for weeping.   205
EYRE
Peace, you cracked groats, you mustard tokens; disquiet not
the brave soldier. Go thy ways, Ralph.
JANE
Ay, ay, you bid him go; what shall I do when he is gone?
FIRK
Why, be doing with me, or my fellow Hodge – be not idle!
EYRE
Let me see thy hand, Jane. This fine hand, this white hand,   210
these pretty fingers must spin, must card, must work.
Work, you bombast-cotton-candle quean, work for your
living, with a pox to you. Hold thee, Ralph, here's five

---

201 *there is* ed. (theres Q1)
205 as verse, ed. (prose in Q1)

---

195 *pickthank* sycophantic
200 *colours* regimental standard
206 *groats* fourpenny coins, unfit for circulation when damaged
      mustard tokens substitute coins used as small change
211 *card* comb wool to make it ready for spinning
212 *bombast-cotton-candle quean* i.e., delicate wench (*bombast* is cotton-wool; good
      candles had cotton wicks); but these refined associations are offset by the
      roughness of tone. Eyre uses the term as general abuse at Scene 7.39. He urges
      Jane to work, presumably, not just for therapeutic reasons but because he has no
      intention of paying Ralph's wages in his absence.
213 *with a pox* with a vengeance, whatever you do. Although he uses the same
      vocabulary as his men, Eyre thinks only of hard work whilst they insinuate that
      Jane should become a prostitute.

sixpences for thee. Fight for the honour of the Gentle
Craft, for the Gentlemen Shoemakers, the courageous   215
cordwainers, the flower of Saint Martin's, the mad knaves
of Bedlam, Fleet Street, Tower Street and Whitechapel.
Crack me the crowns of the French knaves, a pox on
them – crack them! Fight, by the Lord of Ludgate, fight, my
fine boy.   220

FIRK

Here, Ralph, here's three twopences. Two carry into
France, the third shall wash our souls at parting, for sorrow
is dry. For my sake, firk the *basa mon cues*.

HODGE

Ralph, I am heavy at parting, but here's a shilling for thee.
God send thee to cram thy slops with French crowns, and   225
thy enemies' bellies with bullets.

RALPH

I thank you, master, and I thank you all.
Now, gentle wife, my loving, lovely Jane,
Rich men at parting give their wives rich gifts,
Jewels and rings to grace their lily hands.   230
Thou know'st our trade makes rings for women's heels.
Here, take this pair of shoes cut out by Hodge,
Stitched by my fellow Firk, seamed by myself,
Made up and pinked with letters for thy name.
Wear them, my dear Jane, for thy husband's sake,   235
And every morning, when thou pull'st them on,
Remember me, [*Kisses her*] and pray for my return.

216 *cordwainers* shoemakers (the name derives from Cordoba in Spain, a source of
fine leather). Eyre evidently thinks of it as the posh term for his trade.
Saint Martin's the parish of St Martin's-le-Grand, a centre of the shoemaking
trade
217 *Bedlam* Bethlehem Hospital, London's main lunatic asylum just outside
Bishopsgate. Either this is Eyre's joke (punning on *mad*) or the area was another
shoemaking centre.
218 *crowns* heads
222 *wash our souls* buy us a drink
223 *basa mon cues* Firk's pronunciation of *baisez mons culs*, 'kiss-my-arses'
224 *heavy* sad
225 *slops* breeches
French crowns money, but (see line 218) also alluding to heads made bald by
syphilis, which was known as the French disease. Cf. Scene 10. 68–9.
234 *pinked* pricked, decorated

Make much of them, for I have made them so,
That I can know them from a thousand moe.

Sound drum. Enter OATLEY, LINCOLN, LACY, ASKEW,
DODGER, *and soldiers. They pass over the stage,* RALPH *falls
in amongst them,* FIRK *and the rest cry farewell etc., and so
exeunt*

[Scene 2]

Enter ROSE *alone, making a garland*

ROSE
Here sit thou down upon this flow'ry bank,
And make a garland for thy Lacy's head.
These pinks, these roses, and these violets,
These blushing gilliflowers, these marigolds,
The fair embroidery of his coronet,   5
Carry not half such beauty in their cheeks
As the sweet countenance of my Lacy doth.
O my most unkind father! O my stars,
Why loured you so at my nativity
To make me love, yet live robbed of my love?   10
Here as a thief am I imprisonèd
For my dear Lacy's sake, within those walls
Which by my father's cost were builded up
For better purposes. Here must I languish
For him that doth as much lament, I know,   15
Mine absence as for him I pine in woe.

Enter SYBIL

SYBIL
Good morrow, young mistress. I am sure you make that
garland for me, against I shall be Lady of the Harvest.

16 sd (*after* 15, Q1)

---

239 *moe* more. The rhyme underlies the dramatic point of Ralph's reminder and
     signals the close of the scene.
     sd *pass . . . stage* In Dekker's theatre, this was probably a movement from the
     yard to the stage to the yard again, involving a procession through the standing
     audience.
  4 *gilliflowers* wallflowers
 18 *against* for when. Sybil imagines being chosen as harvest-queen.

ROSE

Sybil, what news at London?

SYBIL

None but good. My Lord Mayor your father, and Master   20
Philpot your uncle, and Master Scott your cousin, and
Mistress Frigbottom by Doctors' Commons, do all, by my
troth, send you most hearty commendations.

ROSE

Did Lacy send kind greetings to his love?

SYBIL

O yes, out of cry. By my troth, I scant knew him – here 'a   25
wore a scarf, and here a scarf, here a bunch of feathers, and
here precious stones and jewels, and a pair of garters – O
monstrous! – like one of our yellow silk curtains at home
here in Old Ford House, here in Master Bellymount's
chamber. I stood at our door in Cornhill, looked at him, he   30
at me indeed; spake to him, but he not to me, not a word.
Marry gup, thought I, with a wanion! He passed by me as
proud – Marry, foh! Are you grown humorous? thought
I – and so shut the door, and in I came.

ROSE

O Sybil, how dost thou my Lacy wrong!   35
My Roland is as gentle as a lamb,
No dove was ever half so mild as he.

SYBIL

Mild? Yea, as a bushel of stamped crabs! He looked upon
me as sour as verjuice. Go thy ways, thought I, thou mayst
be much in my gaskins, but nothing in my netherstocks.   40
This is your fault, mistress, to love him that loves not you.
He thinks scorn to do as he's done to, but if I were as you,

25–6 *'a wore a scarf* ed. (a wore scarffe Q1)

---

22 *by* who lives by
   Doctors' Commons lodging-house for lawyers
25 *out of cry* beyond all measure
30 *our . . . Cornhill* i.e., the Oatley town house, as opposed to his country mansion
   at Old Ford, a village to the north-east of London
32 *Marry gup* My, aren't we getting above ourselves?
   wanion vengeance
33 *humorous* moody
38 *bushel* measure of eight gallons
   stamped crabs crab-apples crushed for their sour juice
39 *verjuice* juice of unripe fruit, used in cooking
40 *gaskins . . . netherstocks* breeches . . . stockings; i.e., though I may be out-
   wardly civil to you, don't imagine we are intimate friends

I'd cry: <u>go by, Jeronimo, go by!</u>
I'd set mine old debts against my new driblets,
And the hare's foot against the goose giblets;   45
For if ever I sigh when sleep I should take,
Pray God I may lose my maidenhead when I wake.

ROSE

Will my love leave me then and go to France?

SYBIL

I know not that, but I am sure I see him stalk before the
soldiers. By my troth, he is a proper man, but he is proper   50
that proper doth. Let him go snick up, young mistress.

ROSE

Get thee to London, and learn perfectly
Whether my Lacy go to France or no.
Do this, and I will give thee for thy pains
My cambric apron, and my Romish gloves, *another* *order –*   55
My purple stockings, and a stomacher.
Say, wilt thou do this, Sybil, for my sake?

SYBIL

Will I, quoth 'a! – at whose suit? By my troth, yes, I'll go: a
cambric apron, gloves, a pair of purple stockings, and a
stomacher! I'll sweat in purple, mistress, for you; I'll take   60
anything that comes a' God's name. O rich, a cambric
apron! Faith then, have at uptails all – I'll go jiggy-joggy to
London and be here in a trice, young mistress.   *Exit* [SYBIL]

ROSE

Do so, good Sybil. Meantime wretched I
Will sit and sigh for his lost company.   *Exit*   65

44–7 as verse, ed. (prose in Q1)

43 *Go by, Jeronimo, go by* a hackneyed phrase derived from Kyd's hugely popular
    play *The Spanish Tragedy* (c. 1589), meaning 'be off with you!'
44–5 *I'd ... giblets* proverbial expressions, urging Rose to consider what she's
    letting herself in for
44 *driblets* petty debts
46 *sigh* i.e., for a man
50 *proper* handsome
51 *snick up* hang   55 *cambric* fine linen
56 *stomacher* ornamental covering for the chest, often sewn with jewels
58 *at whose suit* need you ask?
60 *sweat in purple* i.e., be damned for wearing rich clothes
61 *'a God's name* free, for nothing
62 *have ... all* let's get a move on
65 sd *Exit* In Dekker's theatre the transition to Scene 3 would simply involve
    having Rose leave by one door at the rear of the stage as Lacy entered by
    another.

[Scene 3]

Enter ROLAND LACY *like a Dutch shoemaker*

LACY

How many shapes have gods and kings devised
Thereby to compass their desirèd loves!
It is no shame for Roland Lacy then
To clothe his cunning with the Gentle Craft,   *merely following a model –*
That thus disguised I may unknown possess   5
The only happy presence of my Rose.
For her have I forsook my charge in France,
Incurred the King's displeasure, and stirred up
Rough hatred in mine uncle Lincoln's breast.
O love, how powerful art thou, that canst change   10
High birth to bareness, and a noble mind
To the mean semblance of a shoemaker!
But thus it must be: for her cruel father,
Hating the single union of our souls,
Hath secretly conveyed my Rose from London   15
To bar me of her presence; but I trust
Fortune and this disguise will further me
Once more to view her beauty, gain her sight.
Here in Tower Street with Eyre the shoemaker
Mean I a while to work. I know the trade: 20
I learned it when I was in Wittenberg.
Then cheer thy drooping sprites, be not dismayed;
Thou canst not want – do Fortune what she can,
The Gentle Craft is living for a man!   *Exit*

---

11 *bareness* Q1 (baseness *some eds.*)
22 *drooping* ed. (hoping Q1)

---

0 sd *like ... shoemaker* i.e. carrying a shoemaker's tools, and probably in
    traditional Dutch garb of baggy breeches and large felt hat
1 *shapes* disguises, transformations. Lacy refers to Ovid's *Metamorphoses*, one of
    the most popular of Elizabethan books.
4 *cunning ... Craft* The pun anticipates the various ruses that have their origin in
    Eyre's shop.
11 *bareness* poverty. Many editors emend to 'baseness'.
22 *sprites* spirits

[Scene 4]

Enter EYRE, *making himself ready*

EYRE

Where be these boys, these girls, these drabs, these
scoundrels? They wallow in the fat brewis of my bounty,
and lick up the crumbs of my table, yet will not rise to see
my walks cleansed. Come out, you powder-beef queans!
What, Nan! What, Madge Mumblecrust! Come out, you fat   5
midriff-swag-belly whores, and sweep me these kennels,
that the noisome stench offend not the nose of my
neighbours. What, Firk, I say! What, Hodge! Open my shop
windows! What, Firk, I say!

Enter FIRK

FIRK

O master, is't you that speak bandog and bedlam this   10
morning? I was in a dream, and mused what madman was
got into the street so early. Have you drunk this morning,
that your throat is so clear?

EYRE

Ah, well said, Firk; well said, Firk – to work, my fine knave,
to work! Wash thy face, and thou'lt be more blessed.   15

FIRK

Let them wash my face that will eat it – good master, send
for a souse-wife, if you'll have my face cleaner.

Enter HODGE

2 *brewis* broth
3–4 *to ... cleansed* in time to get my walkways cleaned up. The physical detail of
Eyre's speech demands its visual complement in performance; in the 1981 NT
production there was much passing and emptying of chamber-pots.
4 *powder-beef* beef salted for preservation. But Eyre thinks of his women as old
and tough rather than well-preserved.
5 *Madge Mumblecrust* a character in Udall's old play *Ralph Roister Doister*
(c. 1553) whose name betrays her toothlessness
6 *whores* a vague insult, like *queans* in line 4. Both words normally mean
'prostitute.'
kennels gutters, drains
8–9 *shop windows* Elizabethan shop windows had shutters which let down to form
counters; see Introduction, p. xxviii.
10 *speak ... bedlam* is roaring like a mad thing. A *bandog* is a savage watchdog.
16 *Let ... it* i.e., comparing his face to a pig's head being readied for cooking
17 *souse-wife* woman who cleaned and pickled offal

EYRE

Away, sloven! Avaunt, scoundrel! – Good morrow, Hodge; good morrow, my fine foreman.

HODGE

O master, good morrow; you're an early stirrer. Here's a   20
fair morning. Good morrow, Firk. I could have slept this hour. Here's a brave day towards.

EYRE

O haste to work, my fine foreman, haste to work.

FIRK

Master, I am dry as dust to hear my fellow Roger talk of fair weather. Let us pray for good leather, and let clowns   25
and ploughboys, and those that work in the fields, pray for brave days. We work in a dry shop, what care I if it rain?

Enter MARGERY

EYRE

How now, Dame Margery, can you see to rise? Trip and go, call up the drabs your maids.

MARGERY

See to rise! I hope 'tis time enough; 'tis early enough for any   30
woman to be seen abroad. I marvel how many wives in Tower Street are up so soon. God's me, 'tis not noon! Here's a yawling.

EYRE

Peace, Margery, peace. Where's Cicely Bumtrinket your maid? She has a privy fault: she farts in her sleep. Call the   35
quean up. If my men want shoethread, I'll swinge her in a stirrup.

FIRK

Yet that's but a dry beating. Here's still a sign of drought.

22 *brave day towards* fine day ahead
25 *clowns* peasants, labourers
28 *can ... rise?* Eyre's sarcasm: 'is it light enough for you to get up?'
  Trip make haste. *Trip and go* was the name of a morris dance.
31 *marvel* wonder
35 *privy* secret (with an obvious pun on her problem)
36 *want* are without. Presumably it is her job to spin and wax thread ready for shoemaking.
36-7 *swinge ... stirrup* beat her with a strap
38 *dry beating* i.e., one that won't draw blood. Firk will say anything to remind people of his thirst.

Enter LACY [*disguised as* HANS], *singing*

LACY
Der was een bore van Gelderland,
    Frolick sie byen;   40
He was als dronck he could nyet stand,
    Upsee al sie byen;
Tap eens de canneken,
Drincke, schone mannekin.

FIRK
Master, for my life, yonder's a brother of the Gentle Craft.   45
If he bear not Saint Hugh's bones, I'll forfeit my bones.
He's some uplandish workman. Hire him, good master, that
I may learn some gibble-gabble – 'twill make us work the
faster.

EYRE
Peace, Firk. A hard world; let him pass, let him vanish. We   50
have journeymen enough: peace, my fine Firk.

MARGERY
Nay, nay, you're best follow your man's counsel; you shall
see what will come on't. We have not men enough but we
must entertain every butter-box – but let that pass.

HODGE
Dame, 'fore God, if my master follow your counsel he'll   55
consume little beef. He shall be glad of men an' he can
catch them.

FIRK
Ay, that he shall.

---

42 *Upsee al sie* ed. (vpsolce se Q1)   44 *schone* ed. (schoue Q1)

39–44 *Der . . . mannekin* 'There was a boor from Gelderland, merry they be. He
    was so drunk he could not stand; pissed they all be. Fill up the cannikin; drink,
    my fine mannikin.' The Dutchmen had a reputation as drinkers, and 'boer', the
    Dutch word for 'farmer', had already acquired in English the modern sense of
    'boor'.
46 *Saint Hugh's bones* shoemaker's tools, so called after the story of Sir Hugh, who
    became a shoemaker for love of Winifred and was martyred with her, and whose
    bones are discovered and made into tools by a company of shoemakers. The tale
    is told in Deloney's *The Gentle Craft*, ch. 4, where the tools are itemised, and
    dramatised in William Rowley's play *A Shoemaker a Gentleman* (1608).
47 *uplandish* foreign (perhaps with a joking reference to the *Low* Countries)
52 *you're . . . counsel* sarcastic: Margery constantly suspects that her position and
    advice are undermined by Eyre's solidarity with his men. Cf. Scene 7.25 ff., and
    see Introduction, p. xx.
54 *butter-box* common nickname for the Dutch, who were supposedly addicted to
    butter

HODGE

'Fore God, a proper man, and I warrant a fine workman!
Master, farewell; dame, adieu. If such a man as he cannot   60
find work, Hodge is not for you.   *Offer to go*

EYRE

Stay, my fine Hodge.

FIRK

Faith, an' your foreman go, dame, you must take a journey
to seek a new journeyman. If Roger remove, Firk follows.
If Saint Hugh's bones shall not be set a-work, I may prick   65
mine awl in the walls and go play. Fare ye well, master.
Goodbye, dame.

EYRE

Tarry, my fine Hodge, my brisk foreman. Stay, Firk; –
peace, pudding-broth. By the Lord of Ludgate, I love my
men as my life. Peace, you gallimaufry! Hodge, if he want   70
work, I'll hire him. One of you to him – stay, he comes to
us.

LACY

Goeden dach, meester, end you fro, auch.

FIRK

'Nails, if I should speak after him without drinking, I
should choke! And you, friend Oak, are you of the Gentle   75
Craft?

LACY

Yaw, yaw, ik bin den skomawker.

FIRK

Den skomaker, quoth 'a! And hark you, skomaker, have you
all your tools – a good rubbing-pin, a good stopper, a good
dresser, your four sorts of awls, and your two balls of wax,   80
your paring knife, your hand- and thumb-leathers, and
good Saint Hugh's bones to smooth up your work?

---

77   *bin* ed. (vin Q1)

---

70   *gallimaufry* ragbag (literally, a dish of leftovers) – again addressed to Margery
73   *Goeden ... auch* 'Good day, master, and you mistress also'. Lacy's last word is
      spelled 'oak' in Q1, indicating the pronunciation; in line 75 Firk seizes on it as a
      name for the new arrival.
74   *'Nails* God's nails; a common expletive of the period (referring to the nails of
      the Cross) which Firk uses frequently in the play
      after like
77   *Yaw ... skomawker* 'Yes, yes, I am a shoemaker.'

LACY

Yaw, yaw, be neit vorveard. Ik hab al de dingen voour mack
skoes groot end klene.

FIRK

Ha, ha! Good master, hire him. He'll make me laugh so   85
that I shall work more in mirth than I can in earnest.

EYRE

Hear ye, friend: have ye any skill in the mystery of
cordwainers?

LACY

Ik weet niet wat you seg; ik verstaw you niet.

FIRK

Why thus, man. [*He mimes a shoemaker at work*] Ik verste   90
you niet, quoth 'a!

LACY

Yaw, yaw, yaw; ik can dat wel doen.

FIRK

Yaw, yaw – he speaks yawing like a jackdaw that gapes to be
fed with cheese-curds. O, he'll give a villainous pull at a
can of double beer. But Hodge and I have the vantage; we   95
must drink first, because we are the eldest journeymen.

EYRE

What is thy name?

LACY

Hans; Hans Meulter.

EYRE

Give me thy hand, thou'rt welcome. Hodge, entertain him;
Firk, bid him welcome. Come, Hans. Run, wife – bid your   100
maids, your trullibubs, make ready my fine men's break-
fasts. To him, Hodge.

HODGE

Hans, thou'rt welcome. Use thyself friendly, for we are

---

89 *verstaw* ed. (vestaw Q1)

83-4 *Yaw . . . klene* 'Yes, yes, never fear. I have everything for making shoes large
and small.'

87 *mystery* craft

88 *cordwainers* See note on Scene 1.216.

89 *Ik . . . niet* 'I don't know what you say; I cannot understand you.'

92 *Yaw . . . doen* 'Yes, yes, yes; I can do that well.'

93 *jackdaw* Jackdaws were kept as pets.

95 *double* extra-strong

101 *trullibubs* fat guts – combining 'trillibub' (tripe, entrails) with 'trull' (whore; see
note on line 6)

103 *Use thyself* be

good fellows; if not, thou shalt be fought with, wert thou
bigger than a giant.   105
FIRK
Yea, and drunk with, wert thou <u>Gargantua.</u> My master
keeps no cowards, I tell thee. Ho, boy, bring him an
heelblock: here's a new journeyman.

Enter BOY

LACY
O, ik werstaw you: ik moet een halve dossen cans betaelen.
Here, boy, nempt dis skilling, tap eens freelicke.   110
                                                Exit BOY
EYRE
Quick, snipper-snapper, away! Firk, scour thy throat; thou
shalt wash it with Castilian liquor. [*Calls*] Come, my last of
the fives,

Enter BOY

give me a can. Have to thee, Hans! Here, Hodge; here, Firk;
drink, you mad Greeks, and work like true Trojans, and   115
pray for Simon Eyre the shoemaker. Here, Hans; and
thou'rt welcome.
FIRK
Lo, dame, you would have lost a good fellow that will teach
us to laugh. This beer came hopping in well.
MARGERY
Simon, it is almost seven.   120
EYRE
Is't so, Dame Clapperdudgeon? Is't seven o'clock and my
men's breakfast not ready? Trip and go, you soused conger,

106 *Gargantua* a giant in French folklore, generally known in England through
   translations of popular tales rather than through Rabelais' version
108 *heelblock* a small block used to fasten a heel to a shoe, but apparently used here
   as slang for a round of drinks. Perhaps shoemakers kept a tally on their
   heelblocks of rounds bought.
109–10 *O . . . freelicke* 'O, I understand you: I must pay for half a dozen cans. Here,
   boy, take this shilling, fill up once all round.'
112–13 *last . . . fives* last (wooden model of the foot) for small shoes, i.e., little one
121 *Clapperdudgeon* beggar; apparently so called after the wooden clap-dish which
   beggars and lepers beat to indicate their presence. Eyre refers of course to the
   clacking of his wife's tongue.
122 *soused conger* pickled eel

away! Come, you mad Hyperboreans; follow me, Hodge;
follow me, Hans; come after, my fine Firk – to work, to
work a while, and then to breakfast.　　　　　　*Exit* 125

FIRK

Soft, yaw, yaw, good Hans. Though my master have no
more wit but to call you afore me, I am not so foolish to go
behind you, I being the elder journeyman.

　　　　　　　　　　　　　　　　　　Exeunt

[Scene 5]

Holloaing within. Enter WARNER *and* HAMMON *like hunters*

HAMMON

Cousin, beat every brake. The game's not far.
This way with wingèd feet he fled from death
Whilst the pursuing hounds, scenting his steps,
Find out his highway to destruction.
Besides, the miller's boy told me even now　　　　　5
He saw him take soil, and he holloaed him,
Affirming him so embossed
That long he could not hold.

WARNER　　　　　　　　　　　If it be so,
'Tis best we trace these meadows by Old Ford.

A noise of hunters within. Enter BOY

HAMMON

How now, boy, where's the deer? Speak, saw'st thou him?　10

BOY

O yea, I saw him leap through a hedge, and then over a
ditch, then at my Lord Mayor's pale. Over he skipped me,
and in he went me, and 'holloa' the hunters cried, and 'there
boy, there boy'. But there he is, 'a mine honesty.

6 *soil* ed. (saile Q1)

---

123 *Hyperboreans* mythical people who lived beyond the north wind. Eyre may
　　think the description apposite to his happy band of shoemakers, but probably he
　　just likes the sound of the word.
128 *elder* more senior. The new arrival means Firk can pull rank (cf. lines 95–6).
　1 *brake* thicket
　6 *soil* refuge
　7 *embossed* foaming at the mouth from exhaustion
　12 *pale* fence. The reference locates the scene in the vicinity of Old Ford.

HAMMON

    Boy, godamercy. Cousin, let's away.   15

    I hope we shall find better sport today.

                                    Exeunt

[Scene 6]

Hunting within. Enter ROSE *and* SYBIL

ROSE

    Why, Sybil, wilt thou prove a forester?

SYBIL

    Upon some, no! Forester, go by. No, faith, mistress, the
deer came running into the barn through the orchard, and
over the pale. I wot well I looked as pale as a new cheese to
see him, but 'whip!' says Goodman Pinclose, up with his   5
flail, and our Nick with a prong, and down he fell, and they
upon him, and I upon them. By my troth, we had such
sport! And in the end we ended him, his throat we cut,
flayed him, unhorned him, and my Lord Mayor shall eat of
him anon when he comes.   10

Horns sound within

ROSE

    Hark, hark, the hunters come. You're best take heed.

    They'll have a saying to you for this deed.

Enter HAMMON, WARNER, *Huntsmen and Boy*

HAMMON

    God save you, fair ladies.

SYBIL   'Ladies'! O gross!

WARNER

    Came not a buck this way?

ROSE   No, but two does.

  0 sd *Hunting within. Enter* The action is continuous from the previous scene.

  1 *prove* become

  2 *Upon . . . no!* No way!

10 *anon* shortly

12 *have . . . you* have something to say to you, rebuke you

13 *gross* stupid – since only her mistress Rose is a lady

14 *does* i.e., herself and Sybil

HAMMON
  And which way went they? Faith, we'll hunt at those.   15
SYBIL
  At those? Upon some, no! When, can you tell?
WARNER
  Upon some, ay!
SYBIL   Good Lord!
WARNER   'Wounds, then farewell.
HAMMON
  Boy, which way went he?
BOY   This way, sir, he ran.
HAMMON
  This way he ran indeed. Fair Mistress Rose,
  Our game was lately in your orchard seen.   20
WARNER
  Can you advise which way he took his flight?
SYBIL
  Follow your nose, his horns will guide you right.
WARNER
  Thou'rt a mad wench.
SYBIL   O rich!
ROSE   Trust me, not I.
  It is not like the wild forest deer
  Would come so near to places of resort.   25
  You are deceived: he fled some other way.
WARNER
  Which way, my sugar-candy – can you show?
SYBIL
  Come up, good honey-sops; upon some, no!
ROSE
  Why do you stay, and not pursue your game?
SYBIL
  I'll hold my life their hunting nags be lame.   30

16 *When, can you tell?* a proverbial expression of defiance
17 *'Wounds* God's wounds; a common oath
22 *Follow your nose* proverbial. But Sybil also means that the smell of roasting meat will guide him, taunting him with their successful capture of his prey (cf. lines 3–10).
   horns . . . right i.e., instinct will lead men to a horned beast (the comic symbol of cuckoldry)
24 *like* likely
28 *honey-sops* bread soaked in honey. Though a familiar endearment, as a response to Warner's *sugar-candy* it has a satirical ring.

HAMMON
A deer more dear is found within this place.
ROSE
But not the deer, sir, which you had in chase.
HAMMON
I chased the deer; but this dear chaseth me.
ROSE
The strangest hunting that ever I see.
But where's your park?   *She offers to go away*
HAMMON   'Tis here – O, stay!   35
ROSE
Impale me, and then I will not stray.
WARNER
They wrangle, wench: we are more kind than they.
SYBIL
What kind of hart is that dear hart you seek?
WARNER
A heart, dear heart.
SYBIL   Whoever saw the like?
ROSE
To lose your hart, is't possible you can?   40
HAMMON
My heart is lost.
ROSE   Alack, good gentleman.
HAMMON
This poor lost heart would I wish you might find.
ROSE
You by such luck might prove your hart a hind.
HAMMON
Why, luck had horns, so have I heard some say.
ROSE
Now God, an't be his will, send luck into your way!   45

31 *deer more dear* ed. (deere, more deere Q1, *passim*)
38-9 *hart . . . heart* ed. (hart . . . hart Q1)
40 *hart* ed. (heart Q1)

---

31 *deer more dear* This and the *heart/hart* quibble in lines 38–43 are favourite
   motifs in Elizabethan love poetry.
35 sd *offers . . . away* i.e., to go and see his deer park
36 *Impale* put a fence around. Rose warms to the conventional love-combat,
   punning on the sense of 'stick Cupid's arrow in me', with the further bawdy
   implication. If the men are carrying spears the pun is underlined, as is
   Hammon's rather heavy-handed wooing.
37 *kind* loving
44 *luck had horns* i.e., is the *hart* (male deer) – himself – that she *might find*. But
   Hammon's ingenuity opens him to the inevitable cuckold-joke in the next line.

Enter OATLEY *and Servants*

OATLEY
  What, Master Hammon – welcome to Old Ford!
SYBIL
  [*To Warner*] God's pitikins, hands off, sir! – here's my lord.
OATLEY
  I hear you had ill luck, and lost your game.
HAMMON
  'Tis true, my lord.
OATLEY   I am sorry for the same.
  What gentleman is this?
HAMMON   My brother-in-law.   50
OATLEY
  You're welcome both; sith Fortune offers you
  Into my hands, you shall not part from hence
  Until you have refreshed your wearied limbs.
  Go, Sybil, cover the board. You shall be guest
  To no good cheer, but even a hunters' feast.   55
HAMMON
  I thank your lordship. [*Aside to Warner*] Cousin, on my life,
  For our lost venison I shall find a wife.
OATLEY
  In, gentlemen. I'll not be absent long.
                    Exeunt [*all except* OATLEY]
  This Hammon is a proper gentleman,
  A citizen by birth, fairly allied.   60
  How fit an husband were he for my girl!
  Well, I will in, and do the best I can
  To match my daughter to this gentleman.   *Exit*

[Scene 7]

Enter LACY [*disguised as* HANS], *Skipper*, HODGE *and* FIRK

58 sd (*after* 57, Q1)

---

47 *hands off, sir!* Warner has been trying to embrace her.
51 *sith* since
54 *cover the board* lay the table
55 *even a hunters' feast* only a scratch meal, prepared at short notice (see lines
    8–10)
59 *proper* real

SKIPPER

Ik sal you wat seggen, Hans; dis skip dat comen from
Candy is al fol, by Got's sacrament, van sugar, civet,
almonds, cambric, end alle dingen – towsand, towsand ding.
Nempt it, Hans, nempt it vor your meester. Daer be de bils
van laden. Your meester Simon Eyre sal hae good copen.   5
Wat seggen you, Hans?

FIRK

Wat seggen de reggen de copen, slopen? – laugh, Hodge,
laugh!

LACY

Mine liever broder Firk, bringt Meester Eyre tot den signe
van swannekin. Daer sal you find dis skipper end me. Wat   10
seggen you, broder Firk? Doot it, Hodge. Come, skipper.

Exeunt [LACY *and Skipper*]

FIRK

'Bring him', quoth you? Here's no knavery, to bring my
master to buy a ship worth the lading of two or three
hundred thousand pounds. Alas, that's nothing, a trifle, a
bauble, Hodge!   15

HODGE

The truth is, Firk, that the merchant owner of the ship
dares not show his head, and therefore this skipper, that
deals for him, for the love he bears to Hans offers my

9 *tot* ed. (lot Q1)

1–6 *Ik . . . Hans?* 'I'll tell you what, Hans: this ship that came from Candy [Crete]
is absolutely full, by God's sacrament, of sugar, civet, almonds, cambric, and all
things – a thousand, thousand things. Take it, Hans, take it for your master.
There are the bills of lading. Your master Simon Eyre will have a good bargain.
What do you say, Hans?'

2 *civet* animal extract used to make perfume

7 *Wat . . . slopen* an example of Firk's *gibble-gabble* (see Scene 4.48)

9–11 *Mine . . . Hodge* 'My dear brother Firk, bring Master Eyre to the sign of the
Swan. There you shall find this skipper and me. What do you say, brother Firk?
Do it, Hodge.' There were several taverns in London called the Swan, some of
which were known to be frequented by Dutchmen.

13 *worth the lading of* with a cargo worth

13–14 *two . . . pounds* A colossal figure at the time, though in today's money
perhaps a reasonable indication of the cargo's value. Dekker may have written
'two or three hundred' and revised the last word to 'thousand', with the printer
missing the deletion.

17 *dares not show his head* We are not told why, but Dekker may have been
thinking of the expulsion from England in 1597 of Hanseatic merchants, forced
as a consequence to make a quick sale of their remaining goods.

18 *deals* acts as an agent

master Eyre a bargain in the commodities. He shall have a
reasonable day of payment; he may sell the wares by that   20
time, and be an huge gainer himself.

FIRK

Yea, but can my fellow Hans lend my master twenty
porpentines as an earnest-penny?

HODGE

'Portagues' thou wouldst say: here they be, Firk. Hark, they
jingle in my pocket like Saint Mary Overy's bells.   25

Enter EYRE, MARGERY [*and* BOY]

FIRK

Mum, here comes my dame and my master. She'll scold, on
my life, for loitering this Monday. But's all one – let them
all say what they can, Monday's our holiday.

MARGERY

You sing, Sir Sauce, but I beshrew your heart;
I fear for this your singing we shall smart.   30

FIRK

Smart for me, dame? Why, dame, why?

HODGE

Master, I hope you'll not suffer my dame to take down your
journeymen.

FIRK

If she take me down, I'll take her up – yea, and take her
down, too, a buttonhole lower.   35

EYRE

Peace, Firk; not I, Hodge. By the life of Pharaoh, by the
Lord of Ludgate, by this beard, every hair whereof I value
at a king's ransom, she shall not meddle with you. Peace,

19–20 *a reasonable day of payment* fair time in which to raise the money
23 *porpentines* porcupines. Firk is not used to big money; see Scene 1.90 note.
   earnest-penny down-payment
24 *Portagues* These twenty are what Lacy had left after giving Askew part of the
   money received from his uncle (Scene 1.90–108).
25 *Saint Mary Overy's* so called because it was 'over' the river from London; now
   the cathedral of St Saviour, Southwark
28 *Monday's our holiday* Monday was a traditional holiday for shoemakers. Firk
   apparently sings the phrase, perhaps with elaborate repetition.
29 *Sir Sauce* a mock-formal way of saying 'saucy youth'
   beshrew curse
32 *take down* rebuke
34–5 *If . . . lower* i.e., I'll take her down a peg or two. But Firk also spots the
   opportunity for sexual innuendo in Hodge's *take down*.

you bombast-cotton-candle quean – away, Queen of Clubs,
quarrel not with me and my men, with me and my fine Firk.   40
I'll firk you if you do.

MARGERY

Yea, yea, man, you may use me as you please – but let that
pass.

EYRE

Let it pass? Let it vanish away! Peace, am I not Simon
Eyre? Are not these my brave men, brave shoemakers, all   45
gentlemen of the Gentle Craft? Prince am I none, yet am I
nobly born, as being the sole son of a shoemaker. Away,
rubbish. Vanish, melt – melt like kitchen-stuff.

MARGERY

Yea, yea, 'tis well. I must be called rubbish, kitchen-stuff,
for a sort of knaves.   50

FIRK

Nay, dame, you shall not weep and wail in woe for me.
Master, I'll stay no longer. Here's a venentory of my shop-
tools. Adieu, master. Hodge, farewell.

HODGE

Nay, stay, Firk, thou shalt not go alone.

MARGERY

I pray, let them go. There be more maids than Malkin,   55
more men than Hodge, and more fools than Firk.

FIRK

Fools? 'Nails, if I tarry now, I would my guts might be
turned to shoe-thread.

HODGE

And if I stay, I pray God I may be turned to a Turk, and set
in Finsbury for boys to shoot at! Come, Firk.   60

EYRE

Stay, my fine knaves, you arms of my trade, you pillars of
my profession. What, shall a tittle-tattle's words make you

---

44 *pass?* ed. (pass, Q1)

42 *use* another of Margery's quibbles (perhaps inadvertent in this case?),
provoking laughter from the men
46-7 *Prince...shoemaker* Cf. the proverbial motto quoted by Deloney: 'A
Shoemaker's son is a prince born.'
48 *kitchen-stuff* dripping; general refuse from cooking
50 *sort* gang, bunch
52 *venentory* Firk means 'inventory'.
55 *more maids than Malkin* proverbial. Malkin was a common name for a girl.
59-60 *Turk...shoot at* See note to Scene 1.61. Effigies of Turks and other
'infidels' were used as targets.

forsake Simon Eyre? Avaunt, kitchen-stuff! Rip, you
brown-bread tannikin, out of my sight! Move me not. Have
I not ta'en you from selling tripes in Eastcheap, and set you   65
in my shop, and made you hail-fellow with Simon Eyre the
shoemaker? And now do you deal thus with my journeymen? Look, you powder-beef quean, on the face of Hodge:
here's a face for a lord.

FIRK

And here's a face for any lady in Christendom.   70

EYRE

Rip, you chitterling, avaunt! Boy, bid the tapster of the
Boar's Head fill me a dozen cans of beer for my
journeymen.

FIRK

A dozen cans? O brave! Hodge, now I'll stay!

EYRE

[*Aside to* BOY] An' the knave fills any more than two he   75
pays for them.   [*Exit* BOY]
A dozen cans of beer for my journeymen!

[*Enter* BOY *with two cans, and exit*]

Here, you mad Mesopotamians! Wash your livers with this
liquor. Where be the odd ten? No more, Madge, no more.
Well said; drink and to work. What work dost thou, Hodge?   80
What work?

HODGE

I am a-making a pair of shoes for my Lord Mayor's
daughter, Mistress Rose.

FIRK

And I a pair of shoes for Sybil, my Lord's maid. I deal with
her.   85

EYRE

Sybil? Fie, defile not thy fine, workmanly fingers with the

63 *Rip* get out
64 *brown-bread tannikin* Brown bread was despised for its coarseness; *tannikin*
     was a diminutive form of 'Anne', was commonly applied to a Dutch or German
     girl, and could easily become a term of mild abuse.
71 *chitterling* sausage
72 *Boar's Head* probably the tavern of this name in Eastcheap, which was also the
     setting for several scenes in Shakespeare's *Henry IV*
79 *No more, Madge* Perhaps Eyre is reassuring Margery that he is only pretending
     to demand the *odd ten*. Cf. her objection to his largesse at Scene 1.136–7.
80 *Well said* i.e., well done – encouraging them to drink up
84 *deal with* another of Firk's innuendos

feet of kitchen-stuff and basting-ladles! Ladies of the
Court, fine ladies, my lads – commit their feet to our
apparelling. Put gross work to Hans. Yerk and seam, yerk
and seam.   90

FIRK

For yerking and seaming let me alone, an' I come to't.

HODGE

[*Pulling out a money-bag*] Well, master, all this is from the
bias. Do you remember the ship my fellow Hans told you
of? The skipper and he are both drinking at the Swan. Here
be the portagues to give earnest. If you go through with it,   95
you cannot choose but be a lord at least.

FIRK

Nay, dame, if my master prove not a lord, and you a lady,
hang me.

MARGERY

Yea, like enough, if you may loiter and tipple thus.

FIRK

Tipple, dame? No, we have been bargaining with Skellum-   100
Skanderbag-can-you-Dutch-spreaken for a ship of silk
cypress, laden with sugar-candy.

EYRE

Peace, Firk; silence, tittle-tattle. Hodge, I'll go through
with it.

Enter BOY *with a velvet coat and an alderman's gown*

Here's a seal-ring, and I have sent for a guarded gown and a   105
damask cassock. See where it comes – look here, Madgy!
Help me, Firk; apparel me, Hodge.

EYRE *puts it on*

Silk and satin, you mad Philistines, silk and satin!

104, 107 sds (*after* 102, Q1)

---

89 *Yerk* stitch (leather)
92–3 *from the bias* off the point (cf. Scene 1.85 note)
95 *give earnest* put down as advance payment
100–1 *Skellum ... spreaken* i.e., the skipper. Firk's composite name for him is
    routine derogation of the foreigner, although *Skanderbag* was the name of a
    popular hero. *Skellum* (or 'skelm') was a common term for 'thief, rogue'.
102 *cypress ... sugar-candy* Firk has garbled the skipper's account (lines 1–3) of the
    ship's origin and cargo.
105 *guarded* braided

FIRK

Ha, ha! My master will be as proud as a dog in a doublet, all
in beaten damask and velvet.   110

EYRE

Softly, Firk, for rearing of the nap, and wearing threadbare
my garments. How dost thou like me, Firk? How do I look,
my fine Hodge?

HODGE

Why, now you look like yourself, master! I warrant you,
there's few in the city but will give you the wall, and come   115
upon you with the 'Right Worshipful'.

FIRK

'Nails, my master looks like a threadbare cloak new turned
and dressed. Lord, Lord, to see what good raiment doth!
Dame, dame, are you not enamoured?

EYRE

How sayst thou, Madgy? Am I not brisk? Am I not fine?   120

MARGERY

Fine? By my troth, sweetheart, very fine. By my troth, I
never liked thee so well in my life, sweetheart – but let that
pass. I warrant there be many women in the city have not
such handsome husbands, but only for their apparel – but
let that pass, too.   125

Enter LACY *and Skipper*

LACY

Godden day, meester. Dis be de skipper dat heb de skip van
marchandice. De commodity ben good: nempt it, meester,
nempt it.

EYRE

Godamercy, Hans. Welcome, skipper. Where lies this ship
of merchandise?   130

126 sp LACY ed. (Hans Q1, *passim*)

---

109 *as proud as a dog in a doublet* proverbial
111 *for rearing of* in case you raise. Firk is fussing with Eyre's finery.
115 *give you the wall* allow you to pass on the inside
116 *'Right Worshipful'* the proper mode of addressing an alderman
118 *dressed* adorned
120 *brisk* spruce
124 *but only for their apparel* except when they're dressed up. Margery's logic is no
      match for her enthusiasm.
126-8 *Godden . . . nempt it* 'Good day, master. This is the skipper who owns the ship
      of merchandise. The commodity is good: take it, master, take it.'

SKIPPER

De skip ben in revere. Dor be van sugar, civet, almonds, cambric, end a tousand tousand things, Got's sacrament! Nempt it, meester; you sal heb good copen.

FIRK

To him, master. O sweet master! O sweet wares! Prunes, almonds, sugar candy, carrot-roots, turnips – O brave   135 fatting meat! Let not a man buy a nutmeg but yourself.

EYRE

Peace, Firk. Come skipper, I'll go aboard with you. Hans, have you made him drink?

SKIPPER

Yaw, yaw, ik heb veale gedrunck.

EYRE

Come, Hans, follow me. Skipper, thou shalt have my   140 countenance in the city.

                              Exeunt [EYRE, LACY *and Skipper*]

FIRK

Yaw heb veale gedrunck, quotha! They may well be called butter-boxes when they drink fat veal, and thick beer too! But come, dame – I hope you'll chide us no more.

MARGERY

No, faith, Firk. No, perdie, Hodge. I do feel honour creep   145 upon me, and which is more, a certain rising in my flesh – but let that pass.

FIRK

Rising in your flesh do you feel, say you? Ay, you may be with child, but why should not my master feel a rising in his

---

131 *revere* ed. (rouere Q1)
137 *aboard* ed. (abroade Q1)

131-2 *De skip . . . copen* 'The ship is in the river. There are sugar, civet, almonds, cambric, and a thousand thousand things, by God's sacrament! Take it, master; you shall have a good bargain.'

135 *carrot-roots* Firk's mishearing of *cambric*; carrots and turnips were cheap native vegetables.

136 *a nutmeg* i.e., even so small a thing as a nutmeg

138 *made him drink* A courteous enquiry (cf. Scene 11.56) rather than a stealthy aside to Hans, though it is obviously in Eyre's interests to have the skipper well-oiled.

139 *Yaw . . . gedrunck* 'Yes, yes, I have drunk well.'

141 *countenance* protection

149-50 *why . . . on?* Firk sees Eyre's finery as giving him the appearance, and therefore the expectations, of a newly married man.

flesh, having a gown and a gold ring on? But you are such a   150
shrew, you'll soon pull him down.

MARGERY
Ha, ha! Prithee, peace: thou makest my worship laugh – but
let that pass. Come, I'll go in. Hodge, prithee, go before me.
Firk, follow me.

FIRK
Firk doth follow. Hodge, pass out in state!   155

Exeunt

[Scene 8]

Enter LINCOLN *and* DODGER

LINCOLN
How now, good Dodger, what's the news in France?

DODGER
My lord, upon the eighteen day of May
The French and English were prepared to fight.
Each side with eager fury gave the sign
Of a most hot encounter. Five long hours   5
Both armies fought together; at the length
The lot of victory fell on our sides.
Twelve thousand of the Frenchmen that day died,
Four thousand English, and no man of name
But Captain Hyam and young Ardington.   10

LINCOLN
Two gallant gentlemen; I knew them well.
But Dodger, prithee tell me, in this fight
How did my cousin Lacy bear himself?

DODGER
My lord, your cousin Lacy was not there.

LINCOLN
Not there?

DODGER   No, my good lord.

LINCOLN   Sure, thou mistakest: 15

11 sp LINCOLN ed. (Dodger Q1)

---

151 *pull him down* humble (with an obvious quibble)
152 *my worship* Margery is putting on comic airs.
  2 *eighteen* eighteenth
  9 *of name* of the rank of gentleman or above. Dodger's account recalls the
    description of Agincourt in Shakespeare's *Henry V* IV. viii. 102–6.

I saw him shipped, and a thousand eyes beside
Were witnesses of the farewells which he gave
When I with weeping eyes bid him adieu.
Dodger, take heed.
DODGER   My lord, I am advised
That what I spake is true. To prove it so,   20
His cousin Askew, that supplied his place,
Sent me for him from France, that secretly
He might convey himself thither.
LINCOLN   Is't even so?
Dares he so carelessly venture his life
Upon the indignation of a king?   25
Hath he despised my love, and spurned those favours
Which I with prodigal hand poured on his head?
He shall repent his rashness with his soul.
Since of my love he makes no estimate,
I'll make him wish he had not known my hate!   30
Thou hast no other news?
DODGER   None else, my lord.
LINCOLN
None worse I know thou hast. Procure the King
To crown his giddy brows with ample honours,
Send him chief colonel, and all my hope
Thus to be dashed? – but 'tis in vain to grieve.   35
One evil cannot a worse relieve.
Upon my life, I have found out his plot!
That old dog love that fawned upon him so,
Love to that puling girl, his fair-cheeked Rose,
The Lord Mayor's daughter, hath distracted him,   40
And in the fire of that love's lunacy
Hath he burnt up himself, consumed his credit,
Lost the King's love, yea, and I fear his life,
Only to get a wanton to his wife.
Dodger, it is so.
DODGER   I fear so, my good lord.   45

---

23 *thither* ed. (hither Q1)

19 *advised* certain
21 *supplied* took
22 *Sent me ... from France* Sent me from France to fetch him. Askew apparently
has not heeded Lacy's warning at Scene 1.192.
39 *puling* whining
44 *to* for, as

LINCOLN

It is so. – Nay, sure, it cannot be!
I am at my wits' end. Dodger –
DODGER　　　　　　　　　　Yea, my lord?
LINCOLN

Thou art acquainted with my nephew's haunts.
Spend this gold for thy pains; go seek him out.
Watch at my Lord Mayor's: there if he live,　　　　　50
Dodger, thou shalt be sure to meet with him.
Prithee, be diligent. Lacy, thy name
Lived once in honour, now dead in shame!
Be circumspect.　　　　　　　　　　　　　*Exit*
DODGER　　　　　I warrant you, my lord.　　*Exit*

[Scene 9]

Enter OATLEY *and* MASTER SCOTT

OATLEY

Good Master Scott, I have been bold with you
To be a witness to a wedding-knot
Betwixt young Master Hammon and my daughter.

Enter HAMMON *and* ROSE

O, stand aside; see where the lovers come.
ROSE

Can it be possible you love me so?　　　　　　5
No, no, within those eyeballs I espy
Apparent likelihoods of flattery.
Pray now, let go my hand.
HAMMON　　　　　　　　Sweet Mistress Rose,
Misconstrue not my words, nor misconceive
Of my affection, whose devoted soul　　　　　10
Swears that I love thee dearer than my heart.
ROSE

As dear as your own heart? I judge it right:
Men love their hearts best when they're out of sight.
HAMMON

I love you, by this hand.
ROSE　　　　　　　　Yet hands off, now.
If flesh be frail, how weak and frail's your vow!　　15

---

50 *there if he live* Lincoln's suspicion that Oatley might be hiding Lacy is rather
　　odd in view of his perception at Scene 1.71–3.

HAMMON
  Then by my life I swear.
ROSE   Then do not brawl.
  One quarrel loseth wife and life and all.
  Is not your meaning thus?
HAMMON   In faith, you jest.
ROSE
  Love loves to sport; therefore leave love, you're best.
OATLEY
  What, square they, Master Scott?
SCOTT   Sir, never doubt.   20
  Lovers are quickly in and quickly out.
HAMMON
  Sweet Rose, be not so strange in fancying me.
  Nay, never turn aside, shun not my sight.
  I am not grown so fond to found my love
  On any that shall quit it with disdain.   25
  If you will love me, so. If not, farewell.
OATLEY
  Why, how now, lovers, are you both agreed?
HAMMON
  Yes, faith, my lord.
OATLEY   'Tis well. Give me your hand;
  Give me yours, daughter. How now, both pull back?
  What means this, girl?
ROSE   I mean to live a maid.   30
HAMMON
  [*Aside*] But not to die one – pause ere that be said!
OATLEY
  Will you still cross me? Still be obstinate?
HAMMON
  Nay, chide her not, my lord, for doing well.
  If she can live an happy virgin's life,
  'Tis far more blessèd than to be a wife.   35
ROSE
  Say, sir, I cannot. I have made a vow,
  Whoever be my husband, 'tis not you.

16 *brawl* lose your temper. Hammon is getting irritated by Rose's teasing.
20 *square* quarrel
22 *strange in fancying me* contrary, perverse
24 *fond* foolish, besotted
    found confer, bestow. Some editors retain the Q1 spelling *fond* to preserve the play on words.
25 *quit* requite
32 *still* always, persistently

OATLEY
    Your tongue is quick. But Master Hammon, know
    I bade you welcome to another end.
HAMMON
    What, would you have me pule, and pine, and pray,   40
    With 'lovely lady', 'mistress of my heart',
    'Pardon your servant', and the rhymer play,
    Railing on Cupid and his tyrant's dart?
    Or shall I undertake some martial spoil,
    Wearing your glove at tourney and at tilt,   45
    And tell how many gallants I unhorsed?
    Sweet, will this pleasure you?
ROSE   Yea. When wilt begin?
    What, love-rhymes, man? Fie on that deadly sin!
OATLEY
    If you will have her, I'll make her agree.
HAMMON
    Enforcèd love is worse than hate to me.   50
    [*Aside*] There is a wench keeps shop in the Old Change:
    To her will I. It is not wealth I seek;
    I have enough, and will prefer her love
    Before the world. – My good Lord Mayor, adieu.
    Old love for me. I have no luck with new.   *Exit*   55
OATLEY
    Now, mammet, you have well behaved yourself!
    But you shall curse your coyness, if I live.
    Who's within there?

                    [*Enter Servant*]

                    See you convey your mistress
    Straight to th'Old Ford. – I'll keep you strait enough!
    'Fore God, I would have sworn the puling girl   60
    Would willingly accepted Hammon's love.
    But banish him my thoughts. – Go, minion, in.

                    Exit ROSE [*with Servant*]

39 *end* outcome
44 *spoil* exploit
48 *deadly sin!* Rose is mocking Hammon's fastidious refusal to play the courtly
    lover, presumably implying that he hasn't the imagination to do so.
51 *Old Change* a street named after the old Exchange building which was
    superseded in 1566 by Sir Thomas Gresham's Royal Exchange
56 *mammet* little madam
57 *coyness* reluctance
59 *strait* strictly; i.e., I'll cramp your style

{ Now tell me, Master Scott, would you have thought
{ That Master Simon Eyre the shoemaker
{ Had been of wealth to buy such merchandise?   65
SCOTT
    'Twas well, my lord, your honour and myself
    Grew partners with him; for your bills of lading
    Show that Eyre's gains in one commodity
    Rise at the least to full three thousand pound,
    Besides like gain in other merchandise.   70
OATLEY
    Well, he shall spend some of his thousands now,
    For I have sent for him to the Guildhall.

                    Enter EYRE

    See where he comes. Good morrow, Master Eyre.
EYRE
    Poor Simon Eyre, my lord, your shoemaker.
OATLEY
    Well, well, it likes yourself to term you so.   75

                    Enter DODGER

    Now, Master Dodger, what's the news with you?
DODGER
    I'd gladly speak in private to your honour.
OATLEY
    You shall, you shall. Master Eyre and Master Scott,
    I have some business with this gentleman.
    I pray, let me entreat you to walk before   80
    To the Guildhall; I'll follow presently.
    Master Eyre, I hope ere noon to call you sheriff.
EYRE
    I would not care, my lord, if you might call me King of
    Spain. Come, Master Scott.
                    Exeunt [EYRE *and* SCOTT]
OATLEY
    Now, Master Dodger, what's the news you bring?   85
DODGER
    The Earl of Lincoln by me greets your lordship

---

73 *Master* The title recognises that Eyre has become a man of substance; Eyre's
    reply insists that he is still a humble tradesman.
83–4 *I . . . Spain* Perhaps modestly jovial ('I'll believe that when I see it'); but Eyre
    seems to resist Oatley's rather patronising manner.

And earnestly requests you, if you can,
Inform him where his nephew Lacy keeps.

OATLEY
Is not his nephew Lacy now in France?

DODGER
No, I assure your lordship, but disguised   90
Lurks here in London.

OATLEY   London? Is't even so?
It may be, but upon my faith and soul,
I know not where he lives, or whether he lives.
So tell my Lord of Lincoln. Lurch in London?
Well, Master Dodger, you perhaps may start him.   95
Be but the means to rid him into France,
I'll give you a dozen angels for your pains,
So much I love his honour, hate his nephew;
And prithee, so inform thy lord from me.

DODGER
I take my leave.   *Exit*

OATLEY   Farewell, good Master Dodger.   100
Lacy in London? I dare pawn my life
My daughter knows thereof, and for that cause
Denied young Master Hammon in his love.
Well, I am glad I sent her to Old Ford.
God's Lord, 'tis late; to Guildhall I must hie.   105
I know my brethren stay my company.   *Exit*

[Scene 10]

Enter FIRK, [MARGERY,] LACY *and* HODGE

MARGERY
Thou goest too fast for me, Roger. O, Firk –

FIRK
Ay, forsooth.

MARGERY
I pray thee, run – do you hear? – run to Guildhall, and learn

---

1 *O Firk* – ed. (omitted Q1)

---

94 *Lurch* lurk
95 *start* flush him out (metaphor from hunting)
97 *angels* gold coins with the Archangel Michael on one side, worth ten shillings
    (50p). Oatley offers a substantial reward – probably as much as Dodger could
    expect to earn in three months as a servant.

if my husband Master Eyre will take that worshipful
vocation of Master Sheriff upon him. Hie thee, good Firk.   5
FIRK

Take it? Well, I go. An' he should not take it, Firk swears to
forswear him. Yes, forsooth, I go to Guildhall.
MARGERY

Nay, when? Thou art too compendious and tedious.
FIRK

O rare! Your excellence is full of eloquence. [*Aside*] How
like a new cartwheel my dame speaks; and she looks like an   10
old musty ale-bottle going to scalding.
MARGERY

Nay, when! Thou wilt make me melancholy.
FIRK

God forbid your worship should fall into that humour. I
run!   *Exit*
MARGERY

Let me see now, Roger and Hans.   15
HODGE

Ay, forsooth, dame – mistress, I should say, but the old
term so sticks to the roof of my mouth, I can hardly lick it
off.
MARGERY

Even what thou wilt, good Roger. 'Dame' is a fair name for
any honest Christian – but let that pass. How dost thou,   20
Hans?
LACY

Me tank you, fro.
MARGERY

Well, Hans and Roger, you see God hath blessed your
master; and, perdie, if ever he comes to be Master Sheriff
of London – as we are all mortal – you shall see I will have   25
some odd thing or other in a corner for you. I will not be

---

7 *forswear* renounce – i.e., leave
8 *Nay, when* Well, what's keeping you?
  compendious concise – the opposite of what Margery means
10 *like ... speaks* i.e., with a squeaky, affected voice
11 *musty ale-bottle* made of leather, and cleaned by soaking in boiling water. The
   inference is that Margery looks like mutton dressed up as lamb; and, perhaps,
   that she resembles a whore (*scalding* was slang for the hot tub used to treat
   venereal disease).
16 *dame* used only for women of lower rank
21 *Me tank you, fro* 'I thank you, mistress.'
24 *perdie* by God

your back friend – but let that pass. Hans, pray thee, tie my
shoe.

LACY

Yaw, ik sal, fro.

MARGERY

Roger, thou knowest the length of my foot; as it is none of   30
the biggest, so I thank God it is handsome enough. Prithee,
let me have a pair of shoes made: cork, good Roger –
wooden heel too.

HODGE

You shall.

MARGERY

Art thou acquainted with never a farthingale-maker, nor a   35
French-hood maker? I must enlarge my bum – ha, ha! How
shall I look in a hood, I wonder? Perdie, oddly, I think.

HODGE

[Aside] As a cat out of a pillory. – Very well, I warrant you,
mistress.

MARGERY

Indeed, all flesh is grass. And Roger, canst thou tell where I   40
may buy a good hair?

HODGE

Yes, forsooth, at the poulterer's in Gracious Street.

---

38 sp HODGE ed. (Roger Q1, *for remainder of scene*)

---

27 *back friend* false friend. But this and Margery's preceding sentence are open to
bawdy interpretation by Firk.
29 *Yaw, ik sal, fro* 'Yes, I will, mistress.'
30 *knowest ... foot* Apart from its literal meaning, the phrase was proverbial: 'you
know how to win my love', as illustrated by the Cinderella motif in the Ralph-
Jane plot (see Scene 1.232–9). Margery's unintended suggestion stands in
comic contrast to the play's romantic interest.
32–3 *cork ... too* Margery will be teetering in her new shoes, as she asks not only
for high wooden heels but also for cork inner linings which raised the heel in
ordinary shoes.
35 *farthingale* hooped underskirt. In some versions the back half only was stiffened
and was known as a 'bum-roll'.
36 *French-hood* close-fitting pleated hood with round front (hence Hodge's
comment in line 38). All these fashions were particularly associated with
citizens' wives.
38 *cat out* i.e., a whore looking out of the head-hole in a pillory (wooden frame in
which an offender's head and hands were locked)
41 *hair* hair-piece
42 *Gracious Street* Gracechurch Street, also known at this time as 'Grass Street',
which is a guide to Hodge's pronunciation of *Gracious*; this enables him to make
capital out of Margery's irrelevant *all flesh is grass*.

MARGERY

Thou art an ungracious wag. Perdie, I mean a false hair for
my periwig.

HODGE

Why, mistress, the next time I cut my beard you shall have   45
the shavings of it, but they are all true hairs.

MARGERY

It is very hot: I must get me a fan, or else a mask.

HODGE

[*Aside*] So you had need, to hide your wicked face.

MARGERY

Fie upon it, how costly this world's calling is! Perdie, but
that it is one of the wonderful works of God, I would not   50
deal with it. Is not Firk come yet? Hans, be not so sad. Let
it pass and vanish, as my husband's worship says.

LACY

Ik bin frolick; lot see you so.

HODGE

Mistress, will you drink a pipe of tobacco?

MARGERY

O, fie upon it, Roger! Perdie, these filthy tobacco pipes are   55
the most idle, slavering baubles that ever I felt. Out upon it,
God bless us – men look not like men that use them.

Enter RALPH *being lame*

HODGE

What, fellow Ralph! Mistress, look here – Jane's husband!
Why, how now – lame? Hans, make much of him: he's a
brother of our trade, a good workman, and a tall soldier.   60

LACY

You be welcome, broder.

MARGERY

Perdie, I knew him not. How dost thou, good Ralph? I am
glad to see thee well.

47 *fan . . . mask* essential items for the fashionable woman
48 *wicked* ugly
53 *Ik . . . so* 'I am cheerful; let's see you so.'
54 *drink a pipe* the standard Elizabethan term for smoking
56 *idle . . . baubles* useless playthings – with a phallic pun underlined by her choice
   of verb (*felt*)
57 sd *Enter . . . lame* In the 1981 NT production, Ralph threw open the top half of
   a stable door at the back of the set and received a tumultuous welcome. He then
   threw open the lower half to reveal one leg missing.
60 *tall* brave

RALPH

I would God you saw me, dame, as well
As when I went from London into France.   65

MARGERY

Trust me, I am sorry, Ralph, to see thee impotent. Lord,
how the wars have made him sunburnt! The left leg is not
well; 'twas a fair gift of God the infirmity took not hold a
little higher, considering thou camest from France – but let
that pass.   70

RALPH

I am glad to see you well, and I rejoice
To hear that God hath blessed my master so
Since my departure.

MARGERY

Yea truly, Ralph, I thank my maker – but let that pass.

HODGE

And, sirrah Ralph, what news, what news in France?   75

RALPH

Tell me, good Roger, first, what news in England?
How does my Jane? When didst thou see my wife?
Where lives my poor heart? She'll be poor indeed
Now I want limbs to get whereon to feed.

HODGE

Limbs? Hast thou not hands, man? Thou shalt never see a   80
shoemaker want bread, though he have but three fingers on
a hand.

RALPH

Yet all this while I hear not of my Jane.

MARGERY

O Ralph, your wife! Perdie, we know not what's become of
her. She was here a while, and because she was married   85
grew more stately than became her. I checked her, and so
forth. Away she flung, never returned, nor said bye nor bah;
and Ralph, you know: ka me, ka thee. And so as I tell
ye – Roger, is not Firk come yet?

64–5 Ralph is the only character to speak in verse in this scene.

66 *impotent* infirm, weak

67 *sunburnt* stricken. But the secondary sense of 'infected with the pox' (known as
the French disease) prompts Margery's untimely joke in the next line.

80 *Hast thou not hands* (and so are able to work at your trade)

86 *stately* proud, superior

88 *ka me, ka thee* proverbial: one good (or bad) turn deserves another. Margery
attacks Jane's supposed ingratitude to excuse her own lack of interest in what's
become of her.

HODGE

No, forsooth.   90

MARGERY

And so indeed we heard not of her; but I hear she lives in
London – but let that pass. If she had wanted, she might
have opened her case to me or my husband, or to any of my
men; I am sure there's not any of them, perdie, but would
have done her good to his power. Hans, look if Firk be   95
come.

LACY

Yaw, ik sal, fro.   *Exit* LACY

MARGERY

And so, as I said. But Ralph, why dost thou weep? Thou
knowest that naked we came out of our mother's womb,
and naked we must return, and therefore thank God for all   100
things.

HODGE

No, faith, Jane is a stranger here. But Ralph, pull up a good
heart – I know thou hast one. Thy wife, man, is in London.
One told me he saw her a while ago, very brave and neat.
We'll ferret her out, an' London hold her.   105

MARGERY

Alas, poor soul, he's overcome with sorrow. He does but as
I do, weep for the loss of any good thing. But Ralph, get
thee in; call for some meat and drink. Thou shalt find me
worshipful towards thee.

RALPH

I thank you, dame. Since I want limbs and lands,   110
I'll to God, my good friends, and to these my hands. *Exit*

Enter LACY *and* FIRK, *running*

FIRK

Run, good Hans. O Hodge, O mistress! Hodge, heave up
thine ears; mistress, smug up your looks, on with your best
apparel. My master is chosen, my master is called, nay

---

97 *ik* (it Q1)

93 *opened her case* discussed her situation (with a bawdy pun)
97 *Yaw, ik sal, fro* 'Yes, I shall, mistress.'
104 *brave* smartly dressed
109 *worshipful* a benefactor. Margery wants to become Lady Bountiful.
113 *smug* smarten

condemned, by the cry of the country to be sheriff of the 115
City for this famous year now to come and time now being.
A great many men in black gowns were asked for their
voices and their hands, and my master had all their fists
about his ears presently, and they cried Ay, ay, ay, ay; and
so I came away. 120
Wherefore without all other grieve
I do salute you, Mistress Shrieve.

LACY
Yaw, my meester is de groot man, de shrieve.

HODGE
Did not I tell you, mistress? Now I may boldly say 'Good
morrow to your worship'. 125

MARGERY
Good morrow, good Roger. I thank you, my good people
all. Firk, hold up thy hand, here's a threepenny piece for
thy tidings.

FIRK
'Tis but three halfpence, I think. – Yes, 'tis threepence. I
smell the Rose. 130

HODGE
But, mistress, be ruled by me and do not speak so pulingly.

FIRK
'Tis her worship speaks so, and not she. No, faith, mistress,
speak to me in the old key. 'To it, Firk'; 'there, good Firk';
'ply your business, Hodge' – 'Hodge' with a full mouth; 'I'll
fill your bellies with good cheer till they cry twang'. 135

---

115 *condemned* Firk probably means 'confirmed'; but he may be saying that Eyre is
doomed to serve, has no choice in the matter (as was often the case in elections
to civic office).
116 *famous . . . come* perhaps referring (in 1599) to the first year of the coming
century. Firk imitates the manner of an official proclamation.
118 *voices* votes, opinions
119 *presently* immediately, without hesitation
122 *salute* Firk might embrace her (*salute* often meant 'kiss') or make a flourishing
bow.
123 *Yaw . . . shrieve* 'Yes, my master is the great man, the sheriff.'
130 *smell the Rose* a sly pun. The immediate reference is to the rose stamped on
some Elizabethan coins, but as Julia Gasper suggests (*Notes & Queries*, 1985,
p. 59), Margery's tip probably puts Firk in mind of the pub. (There was a
tavern called the Rose near Temple Bar.) Cf. Scene 11.68.
131 *pulingly* unnaturally, affectedly
134 *'Hodge' . . . mouth* i.e., as you used to call him before you started all this 'good
Roger' stuff (see lines 19, 126)

Enter SIMON EYRE *wearing a gold chain*

LACY

  See, myn liever broder, heer compt my meester.

MARGERY

  Welcome home, Master Shrieve. I pray God continue you
  in health and wealth.

EYRE

  See here, my Madgy, a chain, a gold chain for Simon Eyre! I
  shall make thee a lady; here's a French hood for thee. On   140
  with it, on with it – dress thy brows with this flap of a
  shoulder of mutton, to make thee look lovely. Where be my
  fine men? Roger, I'll make over my shop and tools to thee.
  Firk, thou shalt be the foreman. Hans, thou shalt have an
  hundred for twenty. Be as mad knaves as your master Sim 145
  Eyre hath been, and you shall live to be sheriffs of London.
  How dost thou like me, Margery? Prince am I none, yet am
  I princely born! Firk, Hodge, and Hans!

ALL THREE

  Ay, forsooth, what says your worship, Master Sheriff?

EYRE

  Worship and honour, you Babylonian knaves, for the 150
  Gentle Craft! But I forgot myself: I am bidden by my Lord
  Mayor to dinner at Old Ford. He's gone before, I must
  after. Come, Madge, on with your trinkets. Now, my true
  Trojans, my fine Firk, my dapper Hodge, my honest Hans,
  some device, some odd crotchets, some morris or suchlike 155
  for the honour of the gentle shoemakers. Meet me at Old
  Ford; you know my mind.
  Come Madgy, away;
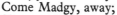
  Shut up the shop, knaves, and make holiday.

                                  Exeunt [EYRE *and* MARGERY]

FIRK

  O rare! O brave! Come, Hodge – follow me, Hans;   160
  We'll be with them for a morris-dance.

                                           Exeunt

---

149 *Master* ed. (mistris Q1)

---

136 *See . . . meester* 'See, my dear brother, here comes my master.'
141–2 *flap . . . mutton* i.e., the French hood
144–5 *an hundred for twenty* i.e., a fivefold return on his loan to Eyre at Scene
    7.22–3
155 *crotchets* entertainments involving music and dance
156 *gentle* gentlemen

[Scene 11]

Enter OATLEY, EYRE, MARGERY *in a French hood,*
[ROSE], SYBIL *and other Servants*

OATLEY
Trust me, you are as welcome to Old Ford
As I myself.
MARGERY   Truly, I thank your lordship.
OATLEY
Would our bad cheer were worth the thanks you give.
EYRE
Good cheer, my Lord Mayor, fine cheer; a fine house, fine
walls, all fine and neat.   5
OATLEY
Now, by my troth, I'll tell thee, master Eyre,
It does me good, and all my brethren,
That such a madcap fellow as thyself
Is entered into our society.
MARGERY
Ay, but, my lord, he must learn now to put on gravity.   10
EYRE
Peace, Madgy, a fig for gravity. When I go to Guildhall in
my scarlet gown I'll look as demurely as a saint, and speak
as gravely as a Justice of Peace; but now I am here at Old
Ford, at my good Lord Mayor's house, let it go by, vanish,
Madgy; I'll be merry. Away with flip-flap, these fooleries, 15
these gulleries. What, honey: prince am I none, yet am I
princely born! What says my Lord Mayor?
OATLEY
Ha, ha, ha! I had rather than a thousand pound
I had an heart but half so light as yours.
EYRE
Why, what should I do, my lord? A pound of care pays not ⌉ 20
a dram of debt. Hum, let's be merry whiles we are young. │
Old age, sack and sugar will steal upon us ere we be aware. ⌋
OATLEY
It's well done. Mistress Eyre, pray give good counsel to my
daughter.

---

12 *scarlet gown* worn by the Lord Mayor and aldermen on ceremonial occasions
16 *gulleries* deceptions; also 'glad rags'
22 *sack and sugar* Sack was already a sweet wine, and old people commonly took it
   with additional sugar.

MARGERY

    I hope Mistress Rose will have the grace to take nothing   25
that's bad.

OATLEY

    Pray God she do, for i'faith, Mistress Eyre,
I would bestow upon that peevish girl
A thousand marks more than I mean to give her
Upon condition she'd be ruled by me.   30
The ape still crosseth me. There came of late
A proper gentleman of fair revenues
Whom gladly I would call son-in-law;
But my fine cockney would have none of him.
You'll prove a coxcomb for it ere you die.   35
A courtier or no man must please your eye.

EYRE

    Be ruled, sweet Rose. Thou'rt ripe for a man: marry not
with a boy that has no more hair on his face than thou hast
on thy cheeks. A courtier? – wash, go by! Stand not upon
pishery-pashery. Those silken fellows are but painted   40
images – outsides, outsides, Rose; their inner linings are
torn. No, my fine mouse, marry me with a Gentleman
Grocer like my Lord Mayor your father. A grocer is a sweet
trade, plums, plums! Had I a son or daughter should marry
out of the generation and blood of the shoemakers, he   45
should pack. What, the Gentle Trade is a living for a man
through Europe, through the world!

A noise within of a tabor and pipe

OATLEY

    What noise is this?

EYRE

    O my Lord Mayor, a crew of good fellows that for love to

29 *marks* A mark was worth two-thirds of a pound.
31 *ape* little monkey
34 *cockney* spoilt child
35 *coxcomb* fool
39 *wash* rubbish (a vague expletive)
40 *pishery-pashery* gaudy rags
42 *mouse* a common term of endearment
46 *pack* go – i.e., I'd turn him out
47 sd *tabor and pipe* small drum and pipe often played by a single performer

your honour are come hither with a morris-dance. [*Calls*]   50
Come in, my Mesopotamians, cheerly!

Enter HODGE, LACY, RALPH, FIRK *and other Shoemakers
in a morris. After a little dancing, the Lord Mayor
speaks*

OATLEY
Master Eyre, are all these shoemakers?
EYRE
All cordwainers, my good Lord Mayor.
ROSE
[*Aside*] How like my Lacy looks yond shoemaker!
LACY
[*Aside*] O, that I durst but speak unto my love!   55
OATLEY
Sybil, go fetch some wine to make these drink. – You are all
welcome.
ALL [THE SHOEMAKERS]
We thank your lordship.

ROSE *takes a cup of wine and goes to* LACY

ROSE
For his sake whose fair shape thou represent'st,
Good friend, I drink to thee.   60
LACY
Ik be dancke, good frister.
MARGERY
I see, Mistress Rose, you do not want judgement. You have
drunk to the properest man I keep.

51 sd *Enter* . . . RALPH Ralph's participation in the dance can be used to generate
pathos (if he is made to fall over or need support), but it also symbolises his full
return to the community. This is an appropriate moment for the first three-
man's song, complementing the dance and reinforcing the festive spirit that
Eyre and his men bring to Oatley's 'bad cheer' (line 3). It also allows Rose more
time to observe the disguised Lacy, especially if he is one of the singers; and a
reprise of the song would be effective as they go out at line 71. See note on the
song (p. 6).
56 *go fetch some wine* Possibly Sybil exits to perform her errand, but a reception
has clearly been laid on and wine could be served from the side or back of the
stage.
59 *whose . . . represent'st* whom you so resemble. Perhaps at this moment Rose
confirms a suspicion that Hans is Lacy.
61 *Ik . . . frister* 'I thank you, good maid.'
62 *want* lack
63 *properest* handsomest

FIRK

    Here be some have done their parts to be as proper as he.

OATLEY

    Well, urgent business calls me back to London.   65
    Good fellows, first go in and taste our cheer,
    And to make merry as you homeward go,
    Spend these two angels in beer at Stratford Bow.

EYRE

    To these two, my mad lads, Sim Eyre adds another. Then
    cheerly, Firk, tickle it, Hans, and all for the honour of   70
    shoemakers.

                    All [*the Shoemakers*] *go dancing out*

OATLEY

    Come, Master Eyre, let's have your company.

                    Exeunt [OATLEY, EYRE *and* MARGERY]

ROSE

    Sybil, what shall I do?

SYBIL   Why, what's the matter?

ROSE

    That Hans the shoemaker is my love, Lacy,
    Disguised in that attire to find me out.   75
    How should I find the means to speak with him?

SYBIL

    What, mistress, never fear. I dare venture my maidenhead
    to nothing – and that's great odds! – that Hans the Dutch-
    man, when we come to London, shall not only see and
    speak with you, but, in spite of all your father's policies,   80
    steal you away and marry you. Will not this please you?

ROSE

    Do this, and ever be assured of my love.

SYBIL

    Away then, and follow your father to London, lest your
    absence cause him to suspect something.
    Tomorrow, if my counsel be obeyed,   85
    I'll bind you prentice to the Gentle Trade.

                          [*Exeunt*]

---

64 *Here be some* Firk objects to her elevation of the newcomer. As usual, his
    phrasing is sexually suggestive.

68 *Stratford Bow* a small village outside London, whose tavern was a regular
    stopping place on the road into the city

70 *tickle it* live it up

80 *policies* plans, schemes

[Scene 12]

Enter JANE *in a sempster's shop, working, and* HAMMON,
muffled, at another door. He stands aloof

HAMMON

Yonder's the shop, and there my fair love sits.
She's fair and lovely, but she is not mine.
O would she were! Thrice have I courted her,
Thrice hath my hand been moistened with her hand
Whilst my poor famished eyes do feed on that   5
Which made them famish. I am infortunate:
I still love one; yet nobody loves me.
I muse in other men what women see
That I so want. Fine Mistress Rose was coy,
And this, too curious. O no, she is chaste,   10
And, for she thinks me wanton, she denies
To cheer my cold heart with her sunny eyes.
How prettily she works! O pretty hand!
O happy work! It doth me good to stand
Unseen to see her. Thus I oft have stood   15
In frosty evenings, a light burning by her,
Enduring biting cold only to eye her.
One only look hath seemed as rich to me
As a king's crown, such is love's lunacy.
Muffled I'll pass along, and by that try   20
Whether she know me.

JANE   Sir, what is't you buy?
What is't you lack, sir? Calico, or lawn,
Fine cambric shirts, or bands? What will you buy?

HAMMON

[*Aside*] That which thou wilt not sell. Faith, yet I'll try. –
How do you sell this handkercher?

JANE   Good cheap.   25

---

0 sd *muffled* i.e., to disguise his identity (cf. lines 20–1) and also against the cold
   (cf. line 17)
7 *I still love one* I'm always in love
9 *want* lack
10 *curious* difficult to please
22 *What is't you lack* a familiar seller's cry, here ironically echoing Hammon's
   complaint at lines 8–9
   lawn fine linen
23 *bands* hat-bands, collars, ruffs

HAMMON
And how these ruffs?
JANE   Cheap too.
HAMMON   And how this band?
JANE
Cheap too.
HAMMON   All cheap. How sell you then this hand?
JANE
My hands are not to be sold.
HAMMON   To be given, then.
Nay, faith, I come to buy.
JANE   But none knows when.
HAMMON
Good sweet, leave work a little while; let's play.   30
JANE
I cannot live by keeping holiday.
HAMMON
I'll pay you for the time which shall be lost.
JANE
With me you shall not be at so much cost.
HAMMON
Look how you wound this cloth, so you wound me.
JANE
It may be so.
HAMMON   'Tis so.
JANE   What remedy?   35
HAMMON
Nay faith, you are too coy.
JANE   Let go my hand.
HAMMON
I will do any task at your command.
I would let go this beauty, were I not
Enjoined to disobey you by a power
That controls kings. I love you.
JANE   So; now part.   40
HAMMON
With hands I may, but never with my heart.
In faith, I love you.
JANE   I believe you do.

_____

39 _Enjoined_ ed. (In mind Q1)

_____

34 _Look how you wound_ just as you prick (with your needle)
39 _Enjoined_ compelled

HAMMON
　Shall a true love in me breed hate in you?
JANE
　I hate you not.
HAMMON　　　　　　Then you must love.
JANE　　　　　　　　　　　　　　　　I do.
　What, are you better now? – I love not you.　　　　45
HAMMON
　All this, I hope, is but a woman's fray,
　That means 'come to me' when she cries 'away!'
　In earnest, mistress – I do not jest –
　A true chaste love hath entered in my breast.
　I love you dearly as I love my life.　　　　　　　50
　I love you as a husband loves a wife.
　That, and no other love, my love requires.
　Thy wealth, I know, is little; my desires
　Thirst not for gold. Sweet beauteous Jane, what's mine
　Shall, if thou make myself thine, all be thine.　　55
　Say, judge, what is thy sentence – life or death?
　Mercy or cruelty lies in thy breath.
JANE
　Good sir, I do believe you love me well,
　For 'tis a silly conquest, silly pride
　For one like you – I mean a gentleman –　　　　　60
　To boast that by his love tricks he hath brought
　Such and such women to his amorous lure.
　I think you do not so; yet many do,
　And make it even a very trade to woo.
　I could be coy, as many women be,　　　　　　　65
　Feed you with sunshine smiles and wanton looks;
　But I detest witchcraft. Say that I
　Do constantly believe you constant have –
HAMMON
　Why dost thou not believe me?
JANE　　　　　　　　　　　　　I believe you.
　But yet, good sir, because I will not grieve you　　70
　With hopes to taste fruit which will never fall,
　In simple truth, this is the sum of all:
　My husband lives – at least, I hope he lives.
　Pressed was he to these bitter wars in France.
　Bitter they are to me by wanting him.　　　　　　75

46 *fray* timidity; noise
55 *myself thine* me your husband
59 *silly . . . silly* unworthy . . . foolish
75 *by wanting him* through missing him

I have but one heart, and that heart's his due.
How can I then bestow the same on you?
Whilst he lives, his I live, be it ne'er so poor;
And rather be his wife than a king's whore.

HAMMON
Chaste and dear woman, I will not abuse thee,   80
Although it cost my life if thou refuse me.
Thy husband pressed for France – what was his name?

JANE
Ralph Damport.

HAMMON   Damport? Here's a letter sent
From France to me from a dear friend of mine,
A gentleman of place. Here he doth write   85
Their names that have been slain in every fight.

JANE
I hope death's scroll contains not my love's name.

HAMMON
Cannot you read?

JANE   I can.

HAMMON   Peruse the same.
To my remembrance such a name I read
Amongst the rest. See here.

JANE   Ay me, he's dead,   90
He's dead! If this be true, my dear heart's slain.

HAMMON
Have patience, dear love.

JANE   Hence! hence!

HAMMON   Nay, sweet Jane,
Make not poor sorrow proud with these rich tears.
I mourn thy husband's death because thou mournest.

JANE
That bill is forged – 'tis signed by forgery!   95

HAMMON
I'll bring thee letters sent besides to many
Carrying the like report. Jane, 'tis too true.
Come, weep not. Mourning, though it rise from love,
Helps not the mournèd, yet hurts them that mourn.

JANE
For God's sake, leave me.

85 *place* rank
86 *names... every fight* Hardly possible, since four thousand were reported killed
  (Scene 8.9). As a plot device this is serviceable, but the implausibility does
  make it more difficult to judge whether Hammon deliberately misleads Jane.
95 *bill* document

HAMMON   Whither dost thou turn?   100
  Forget the dead; love them that are alive.
  His love is faded, try how mine will thrive.
JANE
  'Tis now no time for me to think on love.
HAMMON
  'Tis now best time for you to think on love,
  Because your love lives not.
JANE   Though he be dead,   105
  My love to him shall not be burièd.
  For God's sake, leave me to myself alone.
HAMMON
  'Twould kill my soul to leave thee drowned in moan.
  Answer me to my suit, and I am gone.
  Say to me yea or no.
JANE   No.
HAMMON   Then farewell. –   110
  One farewell will not serve; I come again. –
  Come, dry these wet cheeks. Tell me, faith, sweet Jane,
  Yea, or no: once more.
JANE   Once more I say no.
  Once more be gone, I pray, else will I go.
HAMMON
  Nay, then, I will grow rude. By this white hand,   115
  Until you change that cold 'no', here I'll stand,
  Till by your hard heart –
JANE   Nay, for God's love, peace!
  My sorrows by your presence more increase.
  Not that you thus are present; but all grief
  Desires to be alone. Therefore in brief   120
  Thus much I say, and saying bid adieu:
  If ever I wed man it shall be you.
HAMMON
  O blessèd voice! Dear Jane, I'll urge no more.
  Thy breath hath made me rich.
JANE   Death makes me poor.
Exeunt

---

101 *dead* ed. (deede Q1)

---

115 *grow rude* have to be firm with you. He grasps Jane's wrist, more aggressively
   than before (cf. lines 27–36).
119 *that you thus* because you specifically

[Scene 13]

Enter HODGE *at his shop board,* RALPH, FIRK, LACY
and a Boy, at work

ALL
  [*Singing*] *Hey down, a-down, down derry.*
HODGE
  Well said, my hearts! Ply your work today – we loitered
  yesterday. To it, pell-mell, that we may live to be Lord
  Mayors, or aldermen at least.
FIRK
  [*Singing*] *Hey down a-down derry.*   5
HODGE
  Well said, i'faith! How sayst thou, Hans: doth not Firk
  tickle it?
LACY
  Yaw, meester.
FIRK
  Not so, neither. My organ-pipe squeaks this morning for
  want of liquoring. [*Sings*] *Hey down a-down derry.*   10
LACY
  Forware, Firk, tow best un jolly youngster. Hort, ay,
  meester, ik bid you cut me un pair vampies for Meester
  Jeffrey's boots.
HODGE
  Thou shalt, Hans.
FIRK
  Master.   15
HODGE
  How now, boy?
FIRK
  Pray, now you are in the cutting vein, cut me out a pair of

---

11 *Forware* ed. (Forward Q1)
12 *vampies* ed. (vāpres Q1)

---

0 sd *at his shop board* See Introduction, p. xxviii.
1 *Hey ... down-derry* Cf. the second three-man's song, lines 9–10.
2 *Well said* That's the spirit!
11–12 *Forware ... vampies* 'Indeed, Firk, you are a jolly youth. Listen, master, I
    bid you cut me a pair of vamps ...'. A 'vamp' is the front end of the upper shoe.
16 *boy* Hodge jokingly confirms that Firk is his inferior.

counterfeits, or else my work will not pass current. [*Sings*]
Hey down a-down.

HODGE

Tell me, sirs, are my cousin Mistress Priscilla's shoes done?   20

FIRK

Your cousin? No, master, one of your aunts. Hang her, let
her alone.

RALPH

I am in hand with them. She gave charge that none but I
should do them for her.

FIRK

Thou do for her? Then 'twill be a lame doing; and that she   25
loves not. Ralph, thou mightest have sent her to me: in
faith, I would have yerked and firked your Priscilla. [*Sings*]
Hey down a-down derry. – This gear will not hold.

HODGE

How sayst thou, Firk? Were we not merry at Old Ford?

FIRK

How, merry? Why, our buttocks went jiggy-joggy like a   30
quagmire. Well, Sir Roger Oatmeal, if I thought all meal of
that nature, I would eat nothing but bag-puddings.

RALPH

Of all good fortunes, my fellow Hans had the best.

FIRK

'Tis true, because Mistress Rose drank to him.

HODGE

Well, well, work apace. They say seven of the aldermen be   35
dead, or very sick.

---

18 *counterfeits* copies – i.e., do me a pair of similar vamps while you are about it.
But Gilian West (*Notes & Queries*, 1982, 135–6), suggests that Dekker wrote
'counterforts', meaning the piece of stiff leather forming the back part of a shoe
or boot round the heel.
pass current be sound. Firk puns on the idea of forged currency – passing off
Hodge's work as his own.

21 *aunts* whores

25 *lame doing* a bawdy allusion to Ralph's injury, which Firk hints might have
made him impotent

27 *yerked ... Priscilla* had Priscilla sewn up (bawdy)

28 *This ... hold* this won't last out. Firk could be referring to the shoe he's working
on, or more likely to the state of his throat (cf. lines 9–10).

31 *Oatmeal* i.e., Oatley, who fed the shoemakers in Scene 11
all meal every meal (with a pun on the oatmeal used in *bag-puddings*)

35–6 *seven ... sick* The casual, almost brutal way the news is given and received
reflects the reality of widespread sudden death in Elizabethan society; Dekker is
careful not to make this development, which is crucial to his plot, into a climax.

FIRK

I care not, I'll be none.

RALPH

No, nor I; but then my Master Eyre will come quickly to be
Lord Mayor.

Enter SYBIL

FIRK

Whoop! Yonder comes Sybil.   40

HODGE

Sybil! Welcome, i'faith; and how dost thou, mad wench?

FIRK

Sib-whore, welcome to London.

SYBIL

Godamercy, sweet Firk. Good Lord, Hodge, what a
delicious shop you have got! You tickle it, i'faith.

RALPH

Godamercy, Sybil, for our good cheer at Old Ford.   45

SYBIL

That you shall have, Ralph.

FIRK

Nay, by the mass, we had tickling cheer, Sybil. And how the
plague dost thou and Mistress Rose, and my Lord
Mayor? – I put the women in first.

SYBIL

Well, godamercy. But God's me, I forget myself. Where's   50
Hans the Fleming?

FIRK

Hark, butter-box, now you must yelp out some spreaken.

LACY

Vat begey you, vat vod you, frister?

SYBIL

Marry, you must come to my young mistress, to pull on her
shoes you made last.   55

LACY

Vare ben your edle fro? Vare ben your mistress?

53 *you . . . you* ed. (gon . . . gon Q1)
56 *edle* ed. (egle Q1)

---

43 *Godamercy* thanks
46 *That . . . have* perhaps a joking invitation ('Do come again'), which Sybil as
   servant is not in a position to issue
52 *spreaken* double-Dutch
53 *Vat . . . frister?* 'What do you want? What would you, girl?'
56 *Vere . . . mistress* 'Where is your noble lady? Where is your mistress?'

SYBIL
Marry, here at our London house in Cornwall.

FIRK
Will nobody serve her turn but Hans?

SYBIL
No, sir. Come, Hans, I stand upon needles.

HODGE
Why then, Sybil, take heed of pricking.   60

SYBIL
For that, let me alone; I have a trick in my budget. Come,
Hans.

LACY
Yaw, yaw; ik sal mit you gane.

Exeunt LACY *and* SYBIL

HODGE
Go, Hans, make haste again. Come, who lacks work?

FIRK
I, master, for I lack my breakfast. 'Tis munching time, and   65
past.

HODGE
Is't so? Why then, leave work, Ralph. To breakfast. Boy,
look to the tools. Come, Ralph; come, Firk.

Exeunt

[Scene 14]

Enter a Servingman

SERVINGMAN
Let me see, now ... the sign of the Last in Tower Street.
Mass, yonder's the house. [*Calls*] What haw! Who's within?

Enter RALPH

RALPH
Who calls there? What want you, sir?

57 *Cornwall* an alternative form of 'Cornhill' (cf. Scene 2.30)
61 *trick in my budget* Sybil can match the men in bawdy talk.
63 *Yaw ... gane* 'Yes, yes, I will go with you.'
 0 sd *Enter* The action is continuous from the previous scene, with Ralph turning
   back from the summons to breakfast to answer the servingman's call.
 1 *sign of the Last* indicating a shoemaker's shop

SERVINGMAN

Marry, I would have a pair of shoes made for a gentlewoman against tomorrow morning. What, can you do 5 them?

RALPH

Yes, sir; you shall have them. But what length's her foot?

SERVINGMAN

Why, you must make them in all parts like this shoe. But at any hand fail not to do them, for the gentlewoman is to be married very early in the morning. 10

RALPH

How? By this shoe must it be made? By this? Are you sure, sir? By this?

SERVINGMAN

How 'by this'? Am I sure, 'by this'? Art thou in thy wits? I tell thee, I must have a pair of shoes, dost thou mark me? A pair of shoes, two shoes, made by this very shoe, this same 15 shoe, against tomorrow morning by four o'clock. Dost understand me? Canst thou do't?

RALPH

Yes, sir, yes. Ay, ay, I can do it. – By this shoe, you say? I should know this shoe. Yes, sir, yes, by this shoe. I can do't. Four o'clock; well. Whither shall I bring them? 20

SERVINGMAN

To the sign of the Golden Ball in Watling Street. Enquire for one Master Hammon, a gentleman, my master.

RALPH

Yea, sir. By this shoe, you say.

SERVINGMAN

I say Master Hammon at the Golden Ball. He's the bridegroom, and those shoes are for his bride. 25

RALPH

They shall be done. By this shoe. – Well, well, Master Hammon at the Golden Shoe – I would say, the Golden Ball. Very well, very well. But I pray you, sir, where must Master Hammon be married?

SERVINGMAN

At Saint Faith's Church, under Paul's. But what's that to 30 thee? Prithee, dispatch those shoes; and so farewell. *Exit*

---

5 *against* by
8–9 *at any hand* whatever you do
21 *Golden Ball* perhaps a shop sign. Watling Street was a wealthy retail district.
30 *Saint Faith's* a church in the crypt of old St Paul's, used as a parish church by local residents

RALPH

By this shoe, said he. How am I amazed
At this strange accident! Upon my life,
This was the very shoe I gave my wife
When I was pressed for France; since when, alas,   35
I never could hear of her. It is the same,
And Hammon's bride no other but my Jane.

Enter FIRK

FIRK

'Snails, Ralph, thou hast lost thy part of three pots a
countryman of mine gave me to breakfast.

RALPH

I care not. I have found a better thing.   40

FIRK

A thing? Away! Is it a man's thing, or a woman's thing?

RALPH

Firk, dost thou know this shoe?

FIRK

No, by my troth. Neither doth that know me: I have no
acquaintance with it, 'tis a mere stranger to me.

RALPH

Why then, I do: this shoe, I durst be sworn,   45
Once coverèd the instep of my Jane.
This is her size, her breadth. Thus trod my love.
These true-love knots I pricked. I hold my life,
By this old shoe I shall find out my wife.

FIRK

Ha, ha! Old shoe, that wert new – how a murrain came this   50
ague-fit of foolishness upon thee?

RALPH

Thus, Firk: even now here came a servingman;
By this shoe would he have a new pair made,
Against tomorrow morning, for his mistress
That's to be married to a gentleman.   55
And why may not this be my sweet Jane?

FIRK

And why mayst not thou be my sweet ass? Ha, ha!

38 *'Snails* See note to Scene 4.74.
39 *countryman* neighbour
44 *mere* complete
48 *pricked* i.e., a decorative pattern
50 *murrain* plague

RALPH

Well, laugh and spare not. But the truth is this.
Against tomorrow morning I'll provide
A lusty crew of honest shoemakers   60
To watch the going of the bride to church.
If she prove Jane, I'll take her in despite
From Hammon and the devil, were he by.
If it be not my Jane, what remedy?
Hereof am I sure, I shall live till I die,   65
Although I never with a woman lie.   *Exit*

FIRK

Thou lie with a woman, to build nothing but Cripplegates!
Well, God sends fools fortune, and it may be he may light
upon his matrimony by such a device; for wedding and
hanging goes by destiny.   70
                                              Exit

[Scene 15]

Enter LACY *and* ROSE, *arm in arm*

LACY

How happy am I by embracing thee!
O, I did fear such cross mishaps did reign
That I should never see my Rose again.

ROSE

Sweet Lacy, since fair opportunity
Offers herself to further our escape,   5
Let not too over-fond esteem of me
Hinder that happy hour. Invent the means,
And Rose will follow thee through all the world.

LACY

O, how I surfeit with excess of joy,
Made happy by thy rich perfection!   10
But since thou payest sweet interest to my hopes,
Redoubling love on love, let me once more,

---

67 *Cripplegates* Cripplegate was one of the seven gateways in the city walls, so
  called because disabled people (including wounded soldiers) gathered there to
  beg.
69–70 *wedding . . . destiny* proverbial
 2 *cross* adverse
 6 *too over-fond esteem of* excessive concern for (my honour)

Like to a bold-faced debtor, crave of thee
This night to steal abroad, and at Eyre's house,
Who now by death of certain aldermen   15
Is Mayor of London, and my master once,
Meet thou thy Lacy, where, in spite of chance,
Your father's anger, and mine uncle's hate,
Our happy nuptials will we consummate.

Enter SYBIL

SYBIL
O God, what will you do, mistress? Shift for yourself, your   20
father is at hand. He's coming, he's coming! Master Lacy,
hide yourself. In, my mistress! For God's sake, shift for
yourselves.

LACY
Your father come! Sweet Rose, what shall I do?
Where shall I hide me? How shall I escape?   25

ROSE
A man, and want wit in extremity?
Come, come, be Hans still – play the shoemaker.
Pull on my shoe.

Enter OATLEY

LACY   Mass, and that's well remembered.
SYBIL
Here comes your father.
LACY
Forware, metress, 'tis un good skow; it sal vel dute, or ye   30
sal neit betallen.
ROSE
O God, it pincheth me! What will you do?
LACY
[*Aside*] Your father's presence pincheth, not the shoe.

---

17 *chance* ed. (change Q1)
19 *we* ed. (me Q1)
22 *yourself. In* ed. (your selfe in Q1)

---

22 *yourself. In* Q1's punctuation suggests a bawdy innuendo.
26 *want wit in extremity* lack initiative in a crisis
30-1 *Forware . . . betallen* 'Indeed, mistress, 'tis a good shoe; it will do well, or you
shall not pay for it.'

OATLEY
Well done. Fit my daughter well, and she shall please thee
well.   35
LACY
Yaw, yaw, ik weit dat well. Forware, 'tis un good skoe, 'tis
gi-mait van neat's leather – se ever, mine heer.
OATLEY
I do believe it.

Enter a Prentice

What's the news with you?
PRENTICE
Please you, the Earl of Lincoln at the gate
Is newly lighted, and would speak with you.   40
OATLEY
The Earl of Lincoln come to speak with me?
Well, well, I know his errand. Daughter Rose,
Send hence your shoemaker – dispatch, have done.
Syb, make things handsome. Sir boy, follow me.
                              Exeunt [OATLEY, SYBIL *and Prentice*]
LACY
Mine uncle come? O, what may this portend?   45
Sweet Rose, this of our love threatens an end.
ROSE
Be not dismayed at this. Whate'er befall,
Rose is thine own. To witness I speak truth,
Where thou appoints the place I'll meet with thee.
I will not fix a day to follow thee   50
But presently steal hence! Do not reply.
Love which gave strength to bear my father's hate
Shall now add wings to further our escape.
                                                        Exeunt

---

41 *come to speak* ed. (come speake Q1)
44 sd *Exeunt* (Exit Q1)

34-5 *Fit . . . well* Lacy's reply (line 36) confirms a bawdy interpretation of Oatley's
    remark.
36-7 *Yaw . . . heer* 'Yes, yes, I know that well. Indeed, 'tis a good shoe, 'tis made of
    neat's [cow's] leather – just look, my lord.'
51 *presently* immediately. The modern sense of the word is suggested by Rose's
    sedate verse, but the pace does not slacken here: Oatley and Lincoln enter at
    one door as the lovers leave by another.

[Scene 16]

Enter OATLEY *and* LINCOLN

OATLEY
Believe me – on my credit I speak truth –
Since first your nephew Lacy went to France
I have not seen him. It seemed strange to me
When Dodger told me that he stayed behind,
Neglecting the high charge the King imposed.   5
LINCOLN
Trust me, Sir Roger Oatley, I did think
Your counsel had given head to this attempt,
Drawn to it by the love he bears your child.
Here I did hope to find him in your house;
But now I see mine error, and confess   10
My judgement wronged you by conceiving so.
OATLEY
Lodge in my house, say you? Trust me, my lord,
I love your nephew Lacy too too dearly
So much to wrong his honour; and he hath done so
That first gave him advice to stay from France.   15
To witness I speak truth, I let you know
How careful I have been to keep my daughter
Free from all conference or speech of him –
Not that I scorn your nephew, but in love
I bear your honour, lest your noble blood   20
Should by my mean worth be dishonourèd.
LINCOLN
[*Aside*] How far the churl's tongue wanders from his heart!
– Well, well, Sir Roger Oatley, I believe you,
With more than many thanks for the kind love
So much you seem to bear me. But, my lord,   25
Let me request your help to seek my nephew,
Whom, if I find, I'll straight embark for France.
So shall your Rose be free, my thoughts at rest,
And much care die which now lives in my breast.

28 *your . . . my* ed. (my . . . your Q1)
29 *lives* ed. (dies Q1)

7 *head* encouragement
14 *he* i.e., whoever has misled Lacy

Enter SYBIL

SYBIL
  O Lord, help, for God's sake! My mistress, O my young   30
  mistress!
OATLEY
  Where is thy mistress? What's become of her?
SYBIL
  She's gone, she's fled!
OATLEY   Gone? Whither is she fled?
SYBIL
  I know not, forsooth. She's fled out of doors with Hans the
  shoemaker. I saw them scud, scud, scud, apace, apace!   35
OATLEY
  Which way? [*Calls*] What, John! – Where be my men? –
  Which way?
SYBIL
  I know not, an' it please your worship.
OATLEY
  Fled with a shoemaker? Can this be true?
SYBIL
  O Lord, sir, as true as God's in heaven.   40
LINCOLN
  [*Aside*] Her love turned shoemaker! I am glad of this.
OATLEY
  A Fleming butter-box, a shoemaker!
  Will she forget her birth, requite my care
  With such ingratitude? Scorned she young Hammon
  To love a honnikin, a needy knave?   45
  Well, let her fly. I'll not fly after her.
  Let her starve if she will; she's none of mine.
LINCOLN
  Be not so cruel, sir.

Enter FIRK *with shoes*

SYBIL
  [*Aside*]   I am glad she's 'scaped.
OATLEY
  I'll not account of her as of my child.
  Was there no better object for her eyes   50

35 *scud* scuttle off
41 *Her ... shoemaker* Lincoln has not yet penetrated Lacy's disguise (see lines
    119–20), and enjoys the prospect of Oatley's discomfiture.
45 *honnikin* boor

But a foul drunken lubber, swill-belly,
A shoemaker? That's brave!

FIRK
Yea, forsooth, 'tis a very brave shoe, and as fit as a pudding.

OATLEY
How now, what knave is this? From whence comest thou?

FIRK
No knave, sir. I am Firk the shoemaker, lusty Roger's chief   55
lusty journeyman, and I come hither to take up the pretty
leg of sweet Mistress Rose, and thus hoping your worship is
in as good health as I was at the making hereof, I bid you
farewell, Yours, Firk.   [*Starts to leave*]

OATLEY
Stay, stay, sir knave.

LINCOLN   Come hither, shoemaker.   60

FIRK
'Tis happy the knave is put before the shoemaker, or else I
would not have vouchsafed to come back to you. I am
moved, for I stir.

OATLEY
My lord, this villain calls us knaves by craft.

FIRK
Then 'tis by the Gentle Craft, and to call one 'knave' gently   65
is no harm. Sit your worship merry. [*Aside*] Sib, your young
mistress . . . I'll so bob them, now my master, Master Eyre,
is Lord Mayor of London!

OATLEY
Tell me, sirrah, whose man are you?

FIRK
I am glad to see your worship so merry. I have no maw to   70
this gear, no stomach as yet to a red petticoat (*pointing to*
SYBIL).

67 *them* ed. (then Q1)

---

52 *brave* splendid! In reply, Firk pretends to mistake Oatley's sarcasm as sincere
   praise for Rose's shoes.
53 *as fit as a pudding* from the proverb 'as fit as a pudding for a friar's mouth'
57–9 *hoping . . . Firk* parodying the formal conclusion of a letter. Firk is playing for
   time to cover the lovers' escape, knowing he will be called back.
62 *vouchsafed* condescended. Firk means that Lincoln's more polite mode of
   address has mollified him; but he also implies that, having turned back, those
   standing *before* (in front of) him are knaves.
63 *moved . . . stir* Both words pun on the sense of 'angered'.
67 *bob* make fools of
70–1 *maw to this gear* appetite for this baggage

LINCOLN

He means not, sir, to woo you to this maid,
But only doth demand whose man you are.

FIRK

I sing now to the tune of Rogero. Roger, my fellow, is now
my master. 75

LINCOLN

Sirrah, knowest thou one Hans, a shoemaker?

FIRK

Hans, shoemaker? O yes – stay, yes, I have him! I tell you
what – I speak it in secret – Mistress Rose and he are by this
time – no, not so, but shortly are to come over one another
with 'Can you dance the shaking of the sheets?' It is that 80
Hans – [*Aside*] I'll so gull these diggers.

OATLEY

Knowest thou then where he is?

FIRK

Yes, forsooth. Yea, marry.

LINCOLN

Canst thou, in sadness?

FIRK

No, forsooth. No, marry. 85

OATLEY

Tell me, good honest fellow, where he is,
And thou shalt see what I'll bestow of thee.

FIRK

Honest fellow? No, sir; not so, sir. My profession is the
Gentle Craft. I care not for seeing, I love feeling. Let me
feel it here, *aurium tenus*, ten pieces of gold, *genuum tenus*, 90
ten pieces of silver, and then Firk is your man in a new pair
of stretchers.

OATLEY

Here is an angel, part of thy reward
Which I will give thee: tell me where he is.

74 *Rogero* a popular tune
80 *Can...sheets* the opening line of a sixteenth-century ballad, much used in
  bawdy jests
84 *Canst* know (cf. 'ken')
  sadness seriousness
89 *feeling* slang term for a bribe (cf. 'greasing a palm'); plus Firk's usual innuendo
90 *aurium tenus...genuum tenus* up to the ears...up to the knees. Firk will
  adjust the amount of information given to the size of reward offered.
92 *stretchers* 1) shoe stretchers; 2) lies

FIRK

No point. Shall I betray my brother? No. Shall I prove   95
Judas to Hans? No. Shall I cry treason to my corporation?
No. I shall be firked and yerked then. But give me your
angel. Your angel shall tell you.

LINCOLN

Do so, good fellow; 'tis no hurt to thee.

FIRK

Send simpering Sib away.   100

OATLEY

Huswife, get you in.   *Exit* SYBIL

FIRK

Pitchers have ears, and maids have wide mouths. But for
Hans Prans, upon my word, tomorrow morning he and
young Mistress Rose go to this gear. They shall be married
together, by this rush, or else turn Firk to a firkin of butter   105
to tan leather withal.

OATLEY

But art thou sure of this?

FIRK

Am I sure that Paul's Steeple is a handful higher than
London Stone? Or that the Pissing Conduit leaks nothing
but pure Mother Bunch? Am I sure I am lusty Firk? God's   110
nails, do you think I am so base to gull you?

LINCOLN

Where are they married? Dost thou know the church?

FIRK

I never go to church, but I know the name of it. It is a

---

95 *No point* Absolutely not. The rhetorical questions that follow are clearly aimed
at the theatre audience.

96 *corporation* guild, fellow-workers

97 *firked and yerked* given a real going over

104 *gear* business

105 *by this rush* Firk ironically swears by the least valuable thing he can see. Rushes
were used as floor-coverings.
firkin small keg

109 *London Stone* a large stone (now part of the wall of St Swithin's Church,
Cannon Street) that was a well-known landmark
Pissing Conduit Conduits were the fountains at central points which provided
the city's water; this one was named after the slender stream of water it
provided.

110 *Mother Bunch* a famous tavern hostess. Firk insinuates either that her ale is
weak or that he is reminded of it by the colour of the conduit water.

113 *I . . . church* This is in keeping with what we know of Firk (though church-going
was technically compulsory); but he may mean to say '*the* church'.

swearing-church. Stay a while, 'tis Ay, by the – Mass . . . no,
no, 'tis Ay, by my – troth . . . no, nor that; 'tis Ay, by my   115
faith – that, that! 'Tis Ay by my Faith's Church under
Paul's Cross. There they shall be knit like a pair of
stockings in matrimony; there they'll be incony.

LINCOLN
Upon my life, my nephew Lacy walks
In the disguise of this Dutch shoemaker.   120

FIRK
Yes, forsooth.

LINCOLN
Doth he not, honest fellow?

FIRK
No, forsooth, I think Hans is nobody but Hans, no spirit.

OATLEY
My mind misgives me now 'tis so indeed.

LINCOLN
My cousin speaks the language, knows the trade.   125

OATLEY
Let me request your company, my lord.
Your honourable presence may, no doubt,
Refrain their headstrong rashness, when myself,
Going alone, perchance may be o'erborne.
Shall I request this favour?

LINCOLN   This, or what else.   130

FIRK
Then you must rise betimes, for they mean to fall to their
hey-pass-and-repass, pindy-pandy 'which hand will you
have?' very early.

OATLEY
My care shall every way equal their haste.
This night accept your lodging in my house.   135
The earlier shall we stir, and at Saint Faith's

---

114 *swearing-church* one whose name could be used as an oath
118 *incony* well in. The word's origins are unknown, but its probable Elizabethan
    pronunciation ('incunny') has a bawdy attraction for Firk, comparable to the
    potential for innuendo in 'well in'.
121 *Yes, forsooth* Firk is surprised into this admission, which he then withdraws in
    line 123; or else he is being deliberately confusing.
128 *Refrain* restrain
130 *what else* anything else, whatever you ask
131 *betimes* very early
132 *hey-pass-and-repass* conjurer's patter, here referring to the 'trick' of uniting
    two in marriage
    pindy-pandy Cf. handy-dandy.

Prevent this giddy, hare-brained nuptial.
This traffic of hot love shall yield cold gains:
They ban our loves, and we'll forbid their banns.   *Exit*

LINCOLN
At Saint Faith's Church, thou sayst?   140

FIRK
Yes, by their troth.

LINCOLN
Be secret, on thy life.   [*Exit*]

FIRK
Yes, when I kiss your wife! Ha, ha! Here's no craft in the
Gentle Craft. I came hither of purpose with shoes to Sir
Roger's worship, whilst Rose his daughter be cony-catched   145
by Hans. Soft now: these two gulls will be at Saint Faith's
Church tomorrow morning to take Master Bridegroom and
Mistress Bride napping, and they in the meantime shall
chop up the matter at the Savoy. But the best sport is, Sir
Roger Oatley will find my fellow lame Ralph's wife going   150
to marry a gentleman, and then he'll stop her instead of his
daughter. O brave! There will be fine tickling sport. Soft
now, what have I to do? O, I know – now a mess of
shoemakers meet at the Woolsack in Ivy Lane to cozen my
gentleman of lame Ralph's wife, that's true.   155
      Alack, alack,
      Girls, hold out tack,
      For now smocks for this jumbling
      Shall go to wrack.   *Exit*

---

139 sd *Exit* ed. (exeunt Q1)
142 sd *Exit* ed. (omitted Q1)

---

139 *ban* curse, despise
145 *cony-catched* won by a trick. The term means 'exploited' or 'ripped off'; but it is
     Oatley rather than Rose who has been deceived, and *cony* here recalls rather the
     intimate associations of *incony* in line 118.
149 *the Savoy* a paupers' hospital between the Thames and the Strand whose chapel
     was much used for clandestine marriages
153 *mess* group
154 *the Woolsack* a tavern
     cozen (plan how to) trick
157 *hold out tack* be on your guard, stand firm
158 *smocks...jumbling* maidenheads, as a result of this hanky-panky. Firk's
     rhyming jingle has little relation to the action, and is probably part of a song.

[Scene 17]

Enter EYRE, MARGERY, LACY *and* ROSE

EYRE

This is the morning then – stay, my bully, my honest Hans: is it not?

LACY

This is the morning that must make us two
Happy or miserable; therefore if you –

EYRE

Away with these ifs and ans, Hans, and these etceteras. By 5
mine honour, Roland Lacy, none but the King shall wrong
thee. Come, fear nothing. Am not I Sim Eyre? Is not Sim
Eyre Lord Mayor of London? Fear nothing, Rose, let them
all say what they can. [*Sings*] *Dainty, come thou to
me.* – Laughest thou? 10

MARGERY

Good my lord, stand her friend in what thing you may.

EYRE

Why, my sweet Lady Madgy, think you Simon Eyre can
forget his fine Dutch journeyman? No, vah! Fie, I scorn it.
It shall never be cast in my teeth that I was unthankful.
Lady Madgy, thou hadst never covered thy Saracen's head 15
with this French flap, nor loaden thy bum with this
farthingale – 'tis trash, trumpery, vanity! – Simon Eyre had
never walked in a red petticoat, nor wore a chain of gold,
but for my fine journeyman's portagues; and shall I leave
him? No. Prince am I none, yet bear a princely mind. 20

LACY

My lord, 'tis time for us to part from hence.

EYRE

Lady Madgy, Lady Madgy, take two or three of my
piecrust eaters, my buff-jerkin varlets, that do walk in
black gowns at Simon Eyre's heels. Take them, good Lady

---

 1 *stay* Eyre has to restrain Lacy's eagerness (cf. line 21).
   bully mate, comrade
 9–10 *Dainty . . . me* popular ballad tune
11 *stand* be, act as (with bawdy implication)
15 *Saracen's head* referring to the ugly caricature on an inn-sign (and see note to
   Scene 7.59–60); another of Eyre's roughly affectionate insults
16–17 *flap . . . farthingale* See notes to Scene 10.35–6.
18 *red petticoat* the Lord Mayor's scarlet gown
19 *portagues* See note to Scene 1.90.
23 *buff-jerkin varlets* Eyre's irreverent term for the officers now under his command

Madgy, trip and go, my brown Queen of Periwigs, with my   25
delicate Rose and my jolly Roland to the Savoy, see them
linked, countenance the marriage, and when it is done,
cling, cling together, you Hamborow turtle-doves. I'll bear
you out. Come to Simon Eyre, come dwell with me, Hans,
thou shalt eat minced pies and marchpane. Rose, away,   30
cricket. Trip and go, my Lady Madgy, to the Savoy! Hans,
wed and to bed; kiss and away – go, vanish.

MARGERY
Farewell, my lord.

ROSE
Make haste, sweet love.

MARGERY   She'd fain the deed were done.

LACY
Come, my sweet Rose, faster than deer we'll run.   35

They go out

EYRE
Go, vanish, vanish; avaunt, I say. By the Lord of Ludgate,
it's a mad life to be a Lord Mayor. It's a stirring life, a fine
life, a velvet life, a careful life. Well, Simon Eyre, yet set a
good face on it, in the honour of Saint Hugh. Soft, the King
this day comes to dine with me, to see my new buildings.   40
His Majesty is welcome; he shall have good cheer, delicate
cheer, princely cheer. This day my fellow prentices of
London come to dine with me too. They shall have fine
cheer, gentlemanlike cheer. I promised the mad Cappadocians, when we all served at the conduit together, that if ever   45
I came to be Mayor of London, I would feast them all; and
I'll do't, I'll do't, by the life of Pharaoh, by this beard, Sim
Eyre will be no flincher. Besides, I have procured that upon
every Shrove Tuesday, at the sound of the pancake bell, my

---

25 *brown* lusty
27 *countenance* witness
28 *Hamborow* Hamburg (perhaps alluding to Lacy's disguise: Holland and
    Germany were often confused in English minds)
30 *marchpane* marzipan (i.e., you'll live in luxury)
38 *velvet ... careful* Both terms convey Eyre's awareness of the cares and duties of
    rank; 'velvet-jacket' was slang for a mayor.
40 *my new buildings* See Scene 21.129-32.
44-5 *Cappadocians* Another of Eyre's mouth-fillers: cf. Scene 4.123 and note.
45 *served ... together* i.e., as apprentices, fetching water for their masters' houses
49 *pancake bell* the bell for Church on Shrove Tuesday, but with obvious festive
    associations. The day was a traditional apprentices' holiday.

fine dapper Assyrian lads shall clap up their shop windows   50
and away. This is the day, and this day they shall do't, they
shall do't!
Boys, that day are you free; let masters care,
And prentices shall pray for Simon Eyre.   *Exit*

*Shrove
Tuesday*

[Scene 18]

Enter HODGE, FIRK, RALPH, *and five or six shoemakers,
all with cudgels, or such weapons*

HODGE
Come, Ralph. Stand to it, Firk. My masters, as we are the
brave bloods of the shoemakers, heirs apparent to Saint
Hugh, and perpetual benefactors to all good fellows, thou
shalt have no wrong. Were Hammon a king of spades, he
should not delve in thy close without thy sufferance. But   5
tell me, Ralph, art thou sure 'tis thy wife?
RALPH
Am I sure this is Firk? This morning, when I stroked on her
shoes, I looked upon her, and she upon me, and sighed,
asked me if ever I knew one Ralph. Yes, said I. For his sake,
said she – tears standing in her eyes – and for thou art   10
somewhat like him, spend this piece of gold. I took it; my
lame leg and my travel beyond sea made me unknown. All
is one for that. I know she's mine.
FIRK
Did she give thee this gold? O glorious glittering gold! She's
thine own, 'tis thy wife, and she loves thee; for, I'll stand   15
to't, there's no woman will give gold to any man but she
thinks better of him than she thinks of them she gives silver
to. And for Hammon, neither Hammon nor hangman shall
wrong thee in London. Is not our old master Eyre Lord
Mayor? Speak, my hearts!   20

50 *windows* wooden shutters which let down to form shop counters. See note to
   Scene 4.8–9.
 2 *bloods* brotherhood
 4 *king of spades* punning on *delve*, and anticipating Hammon's rich appearance
   (like the figure on playing-cards) in his wedding finery
 5 *delve in thy close* dig in your patch (bawdy)
   sufferance permission
10 *and for* because
18 *Hammon nor hangman* The word-play alludes to Hamon in the Book of
   Esther who was hanged on the gallows he built for his enemy.

ALL
Yes, and Hammon shall know it to his cost.

Enter HAMMON, *his man*, JANE, *and others*

HODGE
Peace, my bullies; yonder they come.

RALPH
Stand to't, my hearts. Firk, let me speak first.

HODGE
No, Ralph, let me. Hammon, whither away so early?

HAMMON
Unmannerly rude slave, what's that to thee?   25

FIRK
To him, sir? Yes, sir, and to me, and others. Good morrow,
Jane, how dost thou? Good Lord, how the world is changed
with you, God be thanked.

HAMMON
Villains, hands off! How dare you touch my love?

SHOEMAKERS
Villains? Down with them! Cry clubs for prentices!   30

HODGE
Hold, my hearts. Touch her, Hammon? Yea, and more than
that, we'll carry her away with us. My masters and
gentlemen, never draw your bird-spits. Shoemakers are
steel to the back, men every inch of them, all spirit.

ALL OF HAMMON'S SIDE
Well, and what of all this?   35

HODGE
I'll show you. Jane, dost thou know this man? 'Tis Ralph, I
can tell thee. Nay, 'tis he, in faith. Though he be lamed by
the wars, yet look not strange, but run to him, fold him
about the neck and kiss him.

JANE
Lives then my husband? O God, let me go!   40
Let me embrace my Ralph.

HAMMON   What means my Jane?

JANE
Nay, what meant you to tell me he was slain?

HAMMON
Pardon me, dear love, for being misled.

---

30 *clubs for prentices* a rallying-cry. Apprentices were notoriously disorderly during
    the Shrove celebrations.

33 *bird-spits* rapiers (mocking the show of resistance by Hammon and his party)

[*To Ralph*] 'Twas rumoured here in London thou wert
   dead.

FIRK
   Thou seest he lives. Lass, go, pack home with him. Now,   45
   Master Hammon, where's your mistress your wife?

SERVANT
   'Swounds, master, fight for her! Will you thus lose her?

SHOEMAKERS
   Down with that creature! Clubs! Down with him!

HODGE
   Hold, hold!

HAMMON
   Hold, fool! Sirs, he shall do no wrong.   50
   Will my Jane leave me thus, and break her faith?

FIRK
   Yea, sir, she must, sir, she shall, sir. What then? Mend it.

HODGE
   Hark, fellow Ralph; follow my counsel. Set the wench in
   the midst, and let her choose her man, and let her be his
   woman.   55

JANE
   Whom should I choose? Whom should my thoughts affect
   But him whom heaven hath made to be my love?
   [*To Ralph*] Thou art my husband, and these humble weeds
   Makes thee more beautiful than all his wealth.
   Therefore I will but put off his attire,   60
   Returning it into the owner's hand,
   And after ever be thy constant wife.

HODGE
   Not a rag, Jane. The law's on our side. He that sows in
   another man's ground forfeits his harvest. Get thee home,
   Ralph; follow him, Jane. He shall not have so much as a   65
   busk-point from thee.

FIRK
   Stand to that, Ralph. The appurtenances are thine own.
   Hammon, look not at her.

SERVANT
   O 'swounds, no!

47 *'Swounds* by God's wounds
48 *creature* creep, miserable specimen
56 *affect* love
58 *humble weeds* working clothes
60 *his attire* i.e., her wedding-clothes, paid for by Hammon
66 *busk-point* corset-lace

FIRK

Bluecoat, be quiet. We'll give you a new livery else. We'll   70
make Shrove Tuesday Saint George's Day for you. Look
not, Hammon; leer not. I'll firk you! For thy head now – one
glance, one sheep's eye, anything at her. Touch not a rag,
lest I and my brethren beat you to clouts.

SERVANT

Come, Master Hammon, there's no striving here.   75

HAMMON

Good fellows, hear me speak; and honest Ralph,
Whom I have injured most by loving Jane,
Mark what I offer thee. Here in fair gold
Is twenty pound. I'll give it for thy Jane.
If this content thee not, thou shalt have more.   80

HODGE

Sell not thy wife, Ralph; make her not a whore.

HAMMON

Say, wilt thou freely cease thy claim in her,
And let her be my wife?

SHOEMAKERS   No, do not, Ralph!

RALPH

Sirrah Hammon, Hammon, <u>dost thou think a shoemaker is</u>
<u>so base to be a bawd to his own wife for commodity?</u> Take   85
thy gold, choke with it! Were I not lame, I would make thee
eat thy words.

FIRK

A shoemaker sell his flesh and blood – O indignity!

HODGE

Sirrah, take up your pelf and be packing.

HAMMON

I will not touch one penny. But in lieu   90
Of that great wrong I offerèd thy Jane,
To Jane and thee I give that twenty pound.
Since I have failed of her, during my life

70-1 *Bluecoat . . . for you* Servants usually wore a blue livery; St George's Day was
when servants traditionally sought new employment (and so changed livery),
and perhaps Firk threatens to get Hammon's man the sack by involving him in a
brawl.

72 *For* i.e., if you value

73 *sheep's eye* amorous look

74 *clouts* rags

75 *no* no point in

85 *commodity* profit. Hammon is apparently pressing the bag of money on Ralph,
who knocks it to the ground.

89 *pelf* filthy money

I vow no woman else shall be my wife.
Farewell, good fellows of the Gentle Trade.   95
Your morning's mirth my mourning day hath made.

Exeunt [HAMMON *and servants*]

FIRK

[*To Servant going out*] Touch the gold, creature, if you
dare! You're best be trudging. Here, Jane, take thou it. Now
let's home, my hearts.

HODGE

Stay, who comes here? Jane, on again with thy mask.   100

Enter LINCOLN, OATLEY *and Servants*

LINCOLN

Yonder's the lying varlet mocked us so.

OATLEY

Come hither, sirrah.

FIRK

Ay sir, I am sirrah. You mean me, do you not?

LINCOLN

Where is my nephew married?

FIRK

Is he married? God give him joy, I am glad of it. They have   105
a fair day, and the sign is in a good planet – Mars in Venus.

OATLEY

Villain, thou told'st me that my daughter Rose
This morning should be married at Saint Faith's.
We have watched there these three hours at the least,
Yet see we no such thing.   110

FIRK

Truly, I am sorry for't. A bride's a pretty thing.

HODGE

Come to the purpose. Yonder's the bride and bridegroom
you look for, I hope. Though you be lords, you are not to
bar by your authority men from women, are you?

OATLEY

See, see, my daughter's masked.

LINCOLN   True; and my nephew,   115
To hide his guilt, counterfeits him lame.

---

96 *Your...made* Hammon's disconsolate remark recalls the antithesis sadly
observed by Jane at Scene 12.124.

100 *mask* Masks were commonly worn by Elizabethan women as protection against
sunburn.

106 *Mars in Venus* i.e., Mars and Venus in conjunction. Firk's astrology is very hazy.

FIRK

Yea, truly, God help the poor couple, they are lame and blind.

OATLEY

I'll ease her blindness.

LINCOLN   I'll his lameness cure.

FIRK

[*Aside to shoemakers*] Lie down, sirs, and laugh! My fellow   120
Ralph is taken for Roland Lacy, and Jane for Mistress
Damask Rose! This is all my knavery.

OATLEY

[*To Jane*] What, have I found you, minion!

LINCOLN [*To Ralph*]   O base wretch!
Nay, hide thy face; the horror of thy guilt
Can hardly be washed off. Where are thy powers?   125
What battles have you made? O yes, I see
Thou fought'st with shame, and shame hath conquered
    thee.
This lameness will not serve.

OATLEY [*To Jane*]   Unmask yourself.

LINCOLN

Lead home your daughter.

OATLEY   Take your nephew hence.

RALPH

Hence? 'Swounds, what mean you? Are you mad? I hope   130
you cannot enforce my wife from me. Where's Hammon?

OATLEY

Your wife?

LINCOLN

What Hammon?

RALPH

Yea, my wife; and therefore the proudest of you that lays
hands on her first, I'll lay my crutch 'cross his pate!   135

FIRK

To him, lame Ralph! – Here's brave sport!

RALPH

Rose call you her? Why, her name is Jane. Look here else.
[*Unmasks her*] Do you know her now?

---

119 *I'll . . . cure* Presumably Lincoln pulls away Ralph's stick or crutch, making him
   fall over; this might be the cue for Firk's next remark.
122 *Damask Rose* a kind of rose
125 *powers* troops
135 *pate* head

LINCOLN
  Is this your daughter?
OATLEY   No, nor this your nephew.
  My Lord of Lincoln, we are both abused   140
  By this base crafty varlet.
FIRK
  Yea, forsooth, no varlet, forsooth, no 'base'; forsooth, I am
  but mean. No 'crafty' neither, but of the Gentle Craft.
OATLEY
  Where is my daughter Rose? Where is my child?
LINCOLN
  Where is my nephew Lacy marrièd?   145
FIRK
  Why, here is good laced mutton, as I promised you.
LINCOLN
  Villain, I'll have thee punished for this wrong.
FIRK
  Punish the journeyman villain, but not the journeyman
  shoemaker.

                            Enter DODGER

DODGER
  My lord, I come to bring unwelcome news.   150
  Your nephew Lacy, and your daughter Rose
  Early this morning wedded at the Savoy,
  None being present but the Lady Mayoress.
  Besides, I learnt among the officers
  The Lord Mayor vows to stand in their defence   155
  'Gainst any that shall seek to cross the match.
LINCOLN
  Dares Eyre the shoemaker uphold the deed?
FIRK
  Yes, sir, shoemakers dare stand in a woman's quarrel, I
  warrant you, as deep as another and deeper too.

142–3 *'base'. . . mean* A musical pun: I am not singing the bass but the middle
    (*mean*) part of a three-part song.
146 *laced mutton* slang for a prostitute, used only for the sake of the quibble on
    Lacy's name
148 *journeyman villain* Another tortuous pun: Firk seems to distinguish between
    the itinerant labourer (the 'villein' who 'journeys'), liable to prosecution as a
    vagrant, and the qualified craftsman like himself (see Scene 1.132 and note).

DODGER

  Besides, his Grace today dines with the Mayor,   160
  Who on his knees humbly intends to fall
  And beg a pardon for your nephew's fault.

LINCOLN

  But I'll prevent him. Come, Sir Roger Oatley,
  The King will do us justice in this cause.
  Howe'er their hands have made them man and wife,   165
  I will disjoin the match, or lose my life.

                        Exeunt [LINCOLN, OATLEY *and* DODGER]

FIRK

  Adieu, Monsieur Dodger! Farewell, fools! Ha, ha! O, if they
  had stayed, I would have so lammed them with flouts! O
  heart! My codpiece point is ready to fly in pieces every time
  I think upon Mistress Rose – but let that pass, as my Lady   170
  Mayoress says.

HODGE

  This matter is answered. Come, Ralph, home with thy wife.
  Come, my fine shoemakers, let's to our master's the new
  Lord Mayor, and there swagger this Shrove Tuesday. I'll
  promise you wine enough, for Madge keeps the cellar.   175

ALL

  O rare! Madge is a good wench.

FIRK

  And I'll promise you meat enough, for simpering Susan
  keeps the larder. I'll lead you to victuals, my brave soldiers;
  follow your captain. O brave! Hark, hark!

                        Bell rings

ALL

  The pancake bell rings, the pancake bell. Tri-lill, my   180
  hearts!

FIRK

  O brave! O sweet bell! O delicate pancakes! Open the
  doors, my hearts, and shut up the windows. Keep in the
  house, let out the pancakes. O rare, my hearts! Let's march

160 *his Grace* the King
168 *lammed them with flouts* wound them up, bombarded them with jibes
169 *codpiece point* lace holding together the front of the breeches
172 *answered* settled
175 *Madge* clearly a servant rather than Eyre's wife
177 *meat* food
183 *Keep in* i.e., lock up

together for the honour of Saint Hugh to the great new hall   185
in Gracious Street corner, which our master the new Lord
Mayor hath built.

RALPH

O, the crew of good fellows that will dine at my Lord
Mayor's cost today!

HODGE

By the Lord, my Lord Mayor is a most brave man. How   190
shall prentices be bound to pray for him and the honour of
the Gentlemen Shoemakers! Let's feed and be fat with my
lord's bounty.

FIRK

O musical bell still! O Hodge, O my brethren! There's
cheer for the heavens – venison pasties walk up and down   195
piping hot like sergeants, beef and brewis comes marching
in dry-fats, fritters and pancakes comes trolling in in
wheelbarrows, hens and oranges hopping in porters'
baskets, collops and eggs in scuttles, and tarts and custards
comes quavering in in malt shovels.   200

Enter more prentices

ALL

Whoop, look here, look here!

HODGE

How now, mad lads, whither away so fast?

1 PRENTICE

Whither? Why, to the great new hall! Know you not why?
The Lord Mayor hath bidden all the prentices in London to
breakfast this morning.   205

ALL

O brave shoemaker! O brave lord of incomprehensible good
fellowship! Hoo, hark you, the pancake bell rings!

Cast up caps

195 *pasties* ed. (pastimes Q1)

---

190 *brave* fine, impressive – with hospitality to match
196 *brewis* broth
197 *dry-fats* barrels (containing dry goods)
199 *collops* bacon
       scuttles dishes
206 *incomprehensible* Cf. the loose modern use of 'incredible'.

FIRK

Nay, more, my hearts; every Shrove Tuesday is our year of
jubilee, and when the pancake bell rings, we are as free as
my Lord Mayor. We may shut up our shops and make   210
holiday. I'll have it called Saint Hugh's Holiday.

ALL

Agreed, agreed! Saint Hugh's Holiday!

HODGE

And this shall continue for ever.

ALL

O brave! Come, come, my hearts – away, away!

FIRK

O eternal credit to us of the Gentle Craft! March fair, my   215
hearts. O rare!

[Scene 19]

[A flourish of trumpets]
Enter KING *and his train over the stage*

KING

Is our Lord Mayor of London such a gallant?

NOBLEMAN

One of the merriest madcaps in your land.
Your Grace will think, when you behold the man,
He's rather a wild ruffian than a Mayor.
Yet thus much I'll ensure your Majesty: 5
In all his actions that concern his state
He is as serious, provident and wise,
As full of gravity amongst the grave
As any Mayor hath been these many years.

KING

I am with child till I behold this huffcap.   10
But all my doubt is, when we come in presence,
His madness will be dashed clean out of countenance.

208–9 *year of jubilee* annual holiday
211 *Saint Hugh's Holiday* On the significance of Firk's naming of the day, see
    Introduction, pp. xxiv–xxv.
  0 sd *over the stage* See note to Scene 1.239 sd.
  6 *state* official position
 10 *with child* bursting, in suspense
    huff-cap swaggerer
 11 *all my doubt is* I suspect that

NOBLEMAN

It may be so, my liege.

KING   Which to prevent,
Let someone give him notice 'tis our pleasure
That he put on his wonted merriment.   15
Set forward.

ALL

On afore!   *Exeunt*

[Scene 20]

Enter EYRE, HODGE, FIRK, RALPH *and other shoemakers,*
all with napkins on their shoulders

EYRE

Come, my fine Hodge, my jolly Gentlemen Shoemakers –
soft, where be these cannibals, these varlets my officers?
Let them all walk and wait upon my brethren, for my
meaning is that none but shoemakers, none but the livery of
my company shall in their satin hoods wait upon the   5
trencher of my sovereign.

FIRK

O my lord, it will be rare!

EYRE

No more, Firk. Come, lively! Let your fellow prentices
want no cheer. Let wine be plentiful as beer, and beer as
water. Hang these penny-pinching fathers, that cram   10
wealth in innocent lamb-skins. Rip, knaves! Avaunt! Look
to my guests.

HODGE

My lord, we are at our wits' end for room. Those hundred
tables will not feast the fourth part of them.

15 *wonted* usual, customary
 2 *cannibals* Eyre has already referred to his officers as *piecrust eaters* (Scene
   17.23); he is now looking out for the *two or three* he told to accompany Margery
   to the Savoy.
 4 *livery* members. The guilds were distinguished on formal occasions by the
   colour of their hoods.
 6 *trencher* plate, i.e., table
 8 *fellow prentices* used loosely for 'co-workers', since Firk is a journeyman (see
   note to Scene 1.132)
11 *innocent lambskins* purses. A traditional term for a miser was 'pennyfather', and
   Eyre underlines the contrast between grasping old age and his own 'youthful'
   largesse.

EYRE

Then cover me those hundred tables again, and again, till   15
all my jolly prentices be feasted. Avoid, Hodge; run, Ralph;
frisk about, my nimble Firk; carouse me fathom healths to
the honour of the shoemakers. Do they drink lively, Hodge?
Do they tickle it, Firk?

FIRK

Tickle it? Some of them have taken their liquor standing so   20
long that they can stand no longer. But for meat, they
would eat it an' they had it.

EYRE

Want they meat? Where's this swag-belly, this greasy
kitchen-stuff cook? Call the varlet to me. Want meat! Firk,
Hodge, lame Ralph, run, my tall men, beleaguer the   25
shambles, beggar all Eastcheap, serve me whole oxen in
chargers, and let sheep whine upon the tables like pigs for
want of good fellows to eat them. Want meat! Vanish, Firk!
Avaunt, Hodge!

the banquet

HODGE

Your lordship mistakes my man Firk. He means their   30
bellies want meat, not the boards; for they have drunk so
much they can eat nothing.

Enter LACY, ROSE *and* MARGERY

MARGERY

Where is my lord?

EYRE

How now, Lady Madgy?

MARGERY

The King's most excellent Majesty is new come; he sends   35
me for thy honour. One of his most worshipful peers bade
me tell thou must be merry, and so forth – but let that pass.

EYRE

Is my sovereign come? Vanish, my tall shoemakers, my
nimble brethren. Look to my guests, the prentices. – Yet
stay a little: how now, Hans? how looks my little Rose?   40

16 *Avoid* get a move on
17 *Carouse . . . healths* drink deep
21 *meat* food
24 *kitchen-stuff* See note to Scene 7.48.
25–6 *beleaguer the shambles* besiege the meat-stalls
27 *chargers* larger serving dishes

LACY

Let me request you to remember me.
I know your honour easily may obtain
Free pardon of the King for me and Rose,
And reconcile me to my uncle's grace.

Simon as
diplomat

EYRE

Have done, my good Hans, my honest journeyman. Look   45
cheerly. I'll fall upon both my knees till they be as hard as
horn but I'll get thy pardon.

MARGERY

Good my lord, have a care what you speak to his Grace.

EYRE

Away, you Islington whitepot! Hence, you hopperarse, you
barley pudding full of maggots, you broiled carbonado!   50
Avaunt, avaunt, avoid, Mephistophilus! Shall Sim Eyre
learn to speak of you, Lady Madgy? Vanish, Mother
Miniver-Cap, vanish! Go, trip and go, meddle with your
partlets and your pishery-pashery, your flews and your
whirligigs! Go, rub, out of mine alley! Sim Eyre knows how   55
to speak to a pope, to Sultan Soliman, to Tamburlaine an'
he were here. And shall I melt, shall I droop before my
sovereign? No! Come, my Lady Madgy; follow me, Hans;
about your business, my frolic freebooters. Firk, frisk
about, and about, and about, for the honour of mad Simon   60
Eyre, Lord Mayor of London.

FIRK

Hey for the honour of the shoemakers!   *Exeunt*

---

52 *learn* ed. (leaue Q1)

---

44 *grace* favour
49 *Islington whitepot* a dish of milk or cream boiled with eggs, flour and spices,
   apparently a favourite with Londoners on local excursions
   hopperarse big-bum. Cf. Scene 10.35–6.
50 *barley pudding* a kind of sausage
   broiled carbonado a piece of meat scored across and grilled
51 *avoid, Mephistophilus* a catch-phrase resulting from the popularity of
   Marlowe's *Dr Faustus*
53 *Miniver-Cap* Margery's cap is trimmed with ermine for the occasion.
54 *partlets* collars
54–5 *flews ... whirligigs* flaps and fripperies
56 *Sultan ... Tamburlaine* the great conquering rulers of the Middle East whose
   exploits were dramatised in popular Elizabethan plays by Marlowe and Kyd
59 *freebooters* pirates (with a pun on 'bootmakers')

[Scene 21]

A long flourish or two. Enter KING, *Nobles*, EYRE, MARGERY,
LACY *and* ROSE. LACY *and* ROSE *kneel*

KING
  Well, Lacy, though the fact was very foul
  Of your revolting from our kingly love
  And your own duty, yet we pardon you.
  Rise, both; and, Mistress Lacy, thank my Lord Mayor
  For your young bridegroom here.   5

EYRE
  So, my dear liege, Sim Eyre and my brethren the
  Gentlemen Shoemakers shall set your sweet Majesty's
  image cheek by jowl by Saint Hugh for this honour you
  have done poor Simon Eyre. I beseech your Grace pardon
  my rude behaviour. I am a handicraftsman, yet my heart is   10
  without craft. I would be sorry at my soul that my boldness
  should offend my King.

KING
  Nay, I pray thee, good Lord Mayor, be even as merry
  As if thou wert among thy shoemakers.
  It does me good to see thee in this humour.   15

EYRE
  Sayst thou me so, my sweet Diocletian? Then, hump!
  Prince am I none, yet am I princely born. By the Lord of
  Ludgate, my liege, I'll be as merry as a pie.

KING
  Tell me in faith, mad Eyre, how old thou art.

EYRE
  My liege, a very boy, a stripling, a younker. You see not a   20
  white hair on my head, not a grey in this beard. Every hair,
  I assure thy Majesty, that sticks in this beard Sim Eyre

---

1 *fact* deed, action. Desertion during wartime is normally punishable by death.
4 *thank ... Mayor* Eyre has pleaded Lacy's cause between the last scene and the
   present one.
11 *craft* guile
16 *Diocletian* one of the Roman Emperors
   hump! Perhaps a call to raise glasses (cf. line 27). At this point in the 1981 NT
   production Eyre sat down next to the King, causing consternation amongst the
   royal attendants.
18 *pie* magpie. The phrase was proverbial.
20 *younker* mere youth

values at the King of Babylon's ransom. Tamar Cham's
beard was a rubbing-brush to't. Yet I'll shave it off and
stuff tennis balls with it to please my bully King.   25

KING
But all this while I do not know your age.

EYRE
My liege, I am six-and-fifty year old, yet I can cry hump
with a sound heart for the honour of Saint Hugh. Mark this
old wench, my King: I danced the shaking of the sheets
with her six-and-thirty years ago, and yet I hope to get two   30
or three young Lord Mayors ere I die. I am lusty still, Sim
Eyre still. Care and cold lodging brings white hairs. My
sweet Majesty, let care vanish. Cast it upon thy nobles. It
will make thee look always young, like Apollo, and cry
hump! – Prince am I none, yet am I princely born.   35

KING
Ha, ha! Say, Cornwall, didst thou ever see his like?

NOBLEMAN
Not I, my lord.

Enter LINCOLN *and* OATLEY

KING   Lincoln, what news with you?

LINCOLN
My gracious lord, have care unto yourself,
For there are traitors here.

ALL   Traitors? Where? Who?

EYRE
Traitors in my house? God forbid! Where be my officers?   40
I'll spend my soul ere my King feel harm.

KING
Where is the traitor, Lincoln?

LINCOLN [*indicating Lacy*]   Here he stands.

KING
Cornwall, lay hold on Lacy. Lincoln, speak:
What canst thou lay unto thy nephew's charge?

LINCOLN
This, my dear liege. Your Grace to do me honour   45

---

23 *Tamar Cham* famous ruler of China, familiar to theatre audiences from a 1596
   play in which he was probably identified on stage by a distinctive beard
29 *danced . . . sheets* Cf. Scene 16.80 and note.
30 *get* beget, father
41 *spend* give up (i.e., 'over my dead body')

Heaped on the head of this degenerous boy
Desertless favours. You made choice of him
To be commander over powers in France;
But he –
KING   Good Lincoln, prithee pause a while.
Even in thine eyes I read what thou wouldst speak.   50
I know how Lacy did neglect our love,
Ran himself deeply, in the highest degree,
Into vile treason.
LINCOLN   Is he not a traitor?
KING
Lincoln, he was; now have we pardoned him.
'Twas not a base want of true valour's fire   55
That held him out of France, but love's desire.
LINCOLN
I will not bear his shame upon my back.
KING
Nor shalt thou, Lincoln. I forgive you both.
LINCOLN
Then, good my liege, forbid the boy to wed
One whose mean birth will much disgrace his bed.   60
KING
Are they not married?
LINCOLN   No, my liege.
BOTH   We are.
KING
Shall I divorce them, then? O, be it far
That any hand on earth should dare untie
The sacred knot knit by God's majesty.
I would not for my crown disjoin their hands   65
That are conjoined in holy nuptial bands.
How sayst thou, Lacy? Wouldst thou lose thy Rose?
LACY
Not for all India's wealth, my sovereign.
KING
But Rose, I am sure, her Lacy would forgo.
ROSE
If Rose were asked that question, she'd say no.   70
KING
You hear them, Lincoln?
LINCOLN   Yea, my liege, I do.

68 *India's* ed. (Indians Q1)

---

46 *degenerous* degenerate   55 *want* lack

KING
  Yet canst thou find i'the heart to part these two?
  Who seeks, besides you, to divorce these lovers?
OATLEY
  I do, my gracious lord. I am her father.
KING
  [*Aside*] Sir Roger Oatley, our last Mayor, I think?   75
NOBLEMAN
  The same, my liege.
KING   Would you offend love's laws?
  Well, you shall have your wills. You sue to me
  To prohibit the match. Soft, let me see:
  You both are married, Lacy, art thou not?
LACY
  I am, dread sovereign.
KING   Then, upon thy life,   80
  I charge thee not to call this woman wife.
OATLEY
  I thank your Grace.
ROSE   O my most gracious lord!   (*Kneel*)
KING
  Nay, Rose, never woo me. I tell you true,
  Although as yet I am a bachelor,
  Yet I believe I shall not marry you.   85
ROSE
  Can you divide the body from the soul,
  Yet make the body live?
KING   Yea, so profound?
  I cannot, Rose; but you I must divide.
  Fair maid, this bridegroom cannot be your bride.
  Are you pleased, Lincoln? Oatley, are you pleased?   90
BOTH
  Yes, my lord.
KING   Then must my heart be eased;
  For, credit me, my conscience lives in pain
  Till these whom I divorced be joined again.
  Lacy, give me thy hand. Rose, lend me thine.
  Be what you would be. Kiss now; so, that's fine.   95
  At night, lovers, to bed. Now, let me see,
  Which of you all mislikes this harmony?
OATLEY
  Will you then take from me my child perforce?

89 *bride* spouse. 'Bride' was used of both sexes at this date.

KING
    Why, tell me, Oatley, shines not Lacy's name
    As bright in the world's eye as the gay beams   100
    Of any citizen?
LINCOLN   Yea, but, my gracious lord,
    I do mislike the match far more than he.
    Her blood is too too base.
KING   Lincoln, no more.
    Dost thou not know that love respects no blood,
    Cares not for difference of birth or state?   105
    The maid is young, well born, fair, virtuous,
    A worthy bride for any gentleman.
    Besides, your nephew for her sake did stoop
    To bare necessity and, as I hear,
    Forgetting honours and all courtly pleasures,   110
    To gain her love became a shoemaker.
    As for the honour which he lost in France,
    Thus I redeem it: Lacy, kneel thee down.

        [LACY *kneels, and* KING *taps him on the shoulder
                    with a sword*]

    Arise, Sir Roland Lacy. Tell me now,
    Tell me in earnest, Oatley, canst thou chide,   115
    Seeing thy Rose a lady and a bride?
OATLEY
    I am content with what your Grace hath done.
LINCOLN
    And I, my liege, since there's no remedy.
KING
    Come on then, all shake hands; I'll have you friends.
    Where there is much love, all discord ends.   120
    What says my mad Lord Mayor to all this love?
EYRE
    O, my liege, this honour you have done to my fine
    journeyman here, Roland Lacy, and all these favours which
    you have shown to me this day in my poor house, will make
    Simon Eyre live longer by one dozen of warm summers   125
    more than he should.
KING
    Nay, my mad Lord Mayor – that shall be thy name –
    If any grace of mine can length thy life,
    One honour more I'll do thee. That new building
    Which at thy cost in Cornhill is erected   130
    Shall take a name from us. We'll have it called

The Leaden Hall, because in digging it
You found the lead that covereth the same.

EYRE
I thank your Majesty.

MARGERY   God bless your Grace.

KING
Lincoln, a word with you.   135

Enter HODGE, FIRK, RALPH *and more shoemakers*

EYRE
How now, my mad knaves! Peace, speak softly. Yonder is
the King.

KING
With the old troop which there we keep in pay
We will incorporate a new supply.
Before one summer more pass o'er my head,   140
France shall repent England was injurèd.
What are all those?

LACY   All shoemakers, my liege,
Sometimes my fellows. In their companies
I lived as merry as an emperor.

KING
My mad Lord Mayor, are all these shoemakers?   145

EYRE
All shoemakers, my liege, all gentlemen of the Gentle
Craft, true Trojans, courageous cordwainers. They all
kneel to the shrine of holy Saint Hugh.

SHOEMAKERS
God save your Majesty!

KING
Mad Simon, would they anything with us?   150

EYRE
[*To shoemakers*] Mum, mad knaves, not a word – I'll do't, I
warrant you. [*Kneels. To King*] They are all beggars, my
liege, all for themselves; and I for them all on both my
knees do entreat that for the honour of poor Simon Eyre

149 SHOEMAKERS ... *Majesty!* ed. (*All* God saue your maiesty all shoomaker Q1)

132 *Leaden Hall* a familiar landmark to Dekker's audience. The naming of Eyre's
building confirms his solid legacy to the present.
143 *Sometimes* formerly
151 *not a word* The shoemakers are obviously anxious to present a petition to the
King.

and the good of his brethren, these mad knaves, your Grace   155
would vouchsafe some privilege to my new Leaden Hall,
that it may be lawful for us to buy and sell leather there two
days a week.

KING

Mad Sim, I grant your suit. You shall have patent
To hold two market days in Leaden Hall.   160
Mondays and Fridays, those shall be the times.
Will this content you?

ALL   Jesus bless your Grace!

EYRE

In the name of these my poor brethren shoemakers, I most
humbly thank your Grace. But before I rise, seeing you are
in the giving vein, and we in the begging, grant Sim Eyre   165
one boon more.

KING

What is it, my Lord Mayor?

EYRE

Vouchsafe to taste of a poor banquet that stands sweetly
waiting for your sweet presence.

KING

I shall undo thee, Eyre, only with feasts.   170
Already have I been too troublesome;
Say, have I not?

EYRE

O my dear King, Sim Eyre was taken unawares upon a day
of shroving which I promised long ago to the prentices of
London.   175
For, an't please your Highness, in time past
I bare the water-tankard, and my coat
Sits not a whit the worse upon my back.
And then upon a morning some mad boys –
It was Shrove Tuesday even as 'tis now –   180
gave me my breakfast, and I swore then by the stopple of
my tankard if ever I came to be Lord Mayor of London, I
would feast all the prentices. This day, my liege, I did it,
and the slaves had an hundred tables five times covered.
They are gone home and vanished.   185

---

168 *banquet* probably a dessert (which *stands sweetly*) rather than an entire meal
174–83 *shroving . . . prentices* See Scene 17.44–6. The mixture of verse and prose in
Eyre's speech is a sign of incomplete revision in Dekker's manuscript.
181 *stopple* bung
182 *tankard* the water-vessel of line 177

Yet add more honour to the Gentle Trade:
Taste of Eyre's banquet, Simon's happy made.
KING
Eyre, I will taste of thy banquet, and will say
I have not met more pleasure on a day.
Friends of the Gentle Craft, thanks to you all.   190
Thanks, my kind Lady Mayoress, for our cheer.
Come, lords, a while let's revel it at home.
When all our sports and banquetings are done,
Wars must right wrongs which Frenchmen have begun.

Exeunt

FINIS